AF270326

Out of the Ballpark

Out of the Ballpark

How to Think About Baseball

DAVID M. HENKIN

OXFORD
UNIVERSITY PRESS

Oxford University Press is a department of the University of Oxford.
It furthers the University's objective of excellence in research, scholarship,
and education by publishing worldwide. Oxford is a registered trade mark of
Oxford University Press in the UK and in certain other countries.

Published in the United States of America by Oxford University Press
198 Madison Avenue, New York, NY 10016, United States of America.

© Oxford University Press 2026

CIP data is on file at the Library of Congress.

ISBN 9780197789551

Printed by Marquis Book Printing, Canada

The manufacturer's authorized representative in the EU for product safety is
Oxford University Press España S.A. of Parque Empresarial San Fernando de Henares,
Avenida de Castilla, 2 – 28830 Madrid (www.oup.es/en or product.safety@oup.com).
OUP España S.A. also acts as importer into Spain of products made by the manufacturer.

For Josh and Daniel (but not their baseball team)

Table of Contents

Acknowledgments

Space constraints and recency bias unavoidably confine these acknowledgments to a tiny fraction of the interlocutors, scholars, colleagues, students, reporters, online commenters, bloggers, and fellow fans who have contributed to this book. But the following smart, knowledgeable, and generous people read drafts, offered comments, answered queries, supplied information, or otherwise helped me think about baseball while I was working on the project: Alex Toledano, Becca Herman, Bob Heuer, Dan Geary, Edward Septimo, Ethan Orlinsky, Hannah Zeavin, James Vernon, Jen Franco Kamenetz, Jennifer Elias, Jimmy Wallenstein, Nao Sato, Rhae Lynn Barnes, Rob Claar, Roy Kreitner, and Zvi Septimus. I am indebted as well to Daniel Henkin, Amy O'Hearn, and Chloé Tuot for enabling, in distinctive ways, my acquisition and use of images. Thanks also to my friend and agent Alison Mackeen, for representing a book far from her area of interest. At Oxford University Press, I benefited immensely from the expertise and guidance of Lucy Randall, Chelsea Hogue, Ponneelan Moorthy, Betty Pessagno, and two anonymous academic reviewers. Finally, there is Nancy Toff, who approached me with the idea for this book years ago and persuaded an editorial board in the United Kingdom that baseball was something worth thinking about.

1

Introduction

Locating Baseball

Baseball pitchers, along with the people who coach, train, evaluate, admire, or heckle them, speak of "locating the baseball." The phrase refers not to finding a lost ball or tracking its movement, but rather to throwing it with pinpoint accuracy to the precise place where a batter is least likely to be able to hit it hard. In accounting for his astonishing ability to achieve better results than the velocity of his fastball might suggest, Greg Maddux (a long-time superstar who retired in 2008) explained that "a lot of pitchers…try to throw harder. Me, I try to locate better."[1]

For other people, both lovers of the game and those perplexed by its peculiar and persistent appeal, who seek the cultural history and meaning of baseball, the challenge lies less in finding one perfect spot to look, but rather in identifying the many different places where the sport has accumulated significance. Literary celebrations of baseball routinely fix their gaze on the ballpark—the iconic stadium and the mostly green field it encases—as the central space where the game and its history are located. Fan memoirs do the same, recalling an author's initial childhood glimpse of a storied arena as the fated or fateful beginning of a love affair. But narrowing in on stadiums, sandlots, and fabled fields of dreams misses a bigger picture. What happens on the field or in the stands in the societies where baseball is played and watched reflects activities in countless other settings. Baseball's history has also unfolded in columns of newsprint, labor negotiations, and childhood rituals. And clues to its character and significance can be found as readily in rulebooks, museum exhibitions, and novels as on the infield dirt or in the bleachers.

Looking at the game through multiple lenses runs counter to how most books about baseball present their subject. In part, this is because baseball has attracted the admiring attention of poets, novelists, and philosophers, whose professions and skills dispose them to distill the game's essence into core metaphors, myths, or life lessons. Baseball is about geometric form, some declare, or baseball is about learning to fail most of the time. It's about teamwork, or living off the clock, or capitalism, or moral accountability. The fact that such claims, among many others, have been artfully advanced and frequently recycled is part of the game's cultural history. The fact that many of those claims are also contradictory (Is it about rectilinear form or circularity? Is it about assigning individual merit or preventing any individual from being able to succeed without aid? Is it about punctuality or timelessness? Is baseball unique among modern team sports, or is it their model?) suggests, however, that the pursuit of an essential meaning may be a fool's errand. Baseball isn't about any one thing, and it shouldn't be reduced to the values ascribed to it by its fans, however observant and poetic they might be. Instead, understanding baseball requires openness to its manifold, sometimes conflicting, characteristics.

At its core, baseball is simply a game with certain characteristic rules, equipment, and playing surfaces. It resembles many other ball-and-stick team games that have showcased skills and entertained competitors and onlookers in different societies and historical periods. More specifically, baseball resembles various children's games, especially a British game called rounders from which it originated, that feature a tossed ball, a stick used to hit (rather than push or carry) the ball, and a circuit of safe-haven waystations around which players run after hitting the ball. It also resembles the older ball-and-stick game of cricket, played in Great

Britain and by British expatriates and immigrants in other lands—including the United States.

Despite those antecedents and resemblances, a distinctive game known as baseball (initially called "base ball") did not emerge in its current form until the second quarter of the nineteenth century, when adults began playing it in the outdoor spaces of several U.S. cities. Many of the basic rules and much of the vocabulary used to describe play coalesced in the 1840s and 1850s in and around New York City. The establishment in 1845 of Alexander Cartwright's Knickerbocker Club, featuring a written constitution that codified game rules, stands as one possible founding moment in baseball history. But it was not until around 1860 that many of those rules (which included arranging the four bases in a diamond configuration—like rounders but unlike cricket and many other bat-and-ball games—and allowing each team three outs rather than one before changing sides) were adopted beyond the New York area. Even at that point, key aspects of the game would seem odd today: batters could be retired (their turns extinguished), for example, if they hit a ball that was caught after a single bounce; pitchers threw underhanded; and batted balls were fielded bare-handedly. Still, despite numerous changes since and many variants today (softball, tee-ball, wiffle ball, aluminum bats, slow pitching), the basic look and structure of baseball games exhibit a great deal of continuity. Baseball fields are instantly identifiable, as is the action on the field. A team of hitters, generally nine, takes turns with the bat. Batters get three opportunities to hit a ball thrown within their reach. Upon hitting the ball to an area within a field of play bounded by two lines emanating from the batting spot at a right angle, hitters are entitled to begin circling the bases counterclockwise, with the ultimate goal of returning to the batting spot and thereby scoring a point (called a "run"). Thwarting their progress are a team of nine defenders, positioned strategically across the field, who can end a batter's turn in a variety of ways. When three batters are retired, the teams switch roles. When each team has taken a requisite number of shifts (generally nine, like the number of fielders and batters on each side) in the field, the team with the most runs wins. This, in a nutshell, is the game of baseball.

One could elaborate a revealing social history or ethnography of the game I just described, much as one could with any other popular game—tag, hide-and-seek, Uno, or beer pong. But analyzing the game itself in this way would not locate its subject, despite frequent assertions to the contrary by journalists, poets, and philosophers. Baseball's boosters often link the game's meaning to its distinctive regulations and rhythms. It is rare, for example, for a game to award points for running circuitously rather than advancing in a linear direction into an opponent's territory. It is even rarer for a game with a ball to allow only the team *without* its possession to score. And baseball is notable (but not unique) among team sports in not using a clock to govern or constrain the game's action—despite recent changes at the professional level that employ the clock to constrain *pauses* in the action.

All of this is beside the point of this book, however, because baseball is not only a game. Unlike tag and Uno, baseball is also a modern spectator sport. Athletic contests have flourished in every society and era; presumably people have always derived pleasure from watching them. But modern spectator sports feature formally organized competitions that generate interest and accumulate meaning over time and beyond the local communities in which they take place.[2] Everything interesting and significant about the impact of baseball over the past two centuries derives from the game's larger status and history as something masses of people watch, follow, document, and discuss. Understanding baseball as a cultural phenomenon is thus less a matter of identifying the rules, vocabulary, and equipment of a game and more a reckoning with a history of structured competition, official recordkeeping, and audience engagement far from the field. Baseball is a set of practices and ideas that have grown up around a spectator sport, which in turn shaped the experience of playing the game recreationally at the most informal levels and in the most private settings. Even the stereotypical backyard game of catch between father and son draws meaning from its associations with the organized sport.

Thinking about baseball as commercial entertainment rather than athletic contest requires resisting the temptation to explain baseball solely in terms of what appears on the field. Many of the most eloquent words that have been uttered about baseball describe what is happening beneath the opaque surfaces of a dense, slow-moving spectacle. But those descriptions typically work best by screening out most of the pressures, impulses, and institutional forces that turn a recreational game into mass entertainment. Taking baseball seriously as entertainment requires bringing those pressures and impulses back into the picture.

The best way to gain perspective on this form of mass entertainment is to track it in multiple places. This is partly a geographical adventure. The story of baseball is centered, unavoidably, in North America, where it originated as popular entertainment. Subsequently, baseball took root mostly in places connected to the United States at some point through imperial conquest, military occupation, political hegemony, or economic exploitation. But that fact is misleading. Cubans began playing and watching baseball when the island was still a Spanish colony. Baseball became a national sport in Japan many decades before the U.S. occupation, and it was the Japanese empire, rather than the American one, that brought baseball to Korea and Taiwan. In the current century of global migration and telecommunication, playing and watching baseball have spread further, though U.S.-based corporations have played an outsized role in promoting this development. It is now likely that most people in the world who pay attention to baseball games live outside the fifty states. Remarkably, the 2024 World Series (pitting teams from New York and Los Angeles) attracted a larger television audience in Japan than in the United States.

Although baseball is by no means a global spectator sport on the level of soccer, it is nonetheless a legible cultural activity in multiple languages and locales.

At the same time, baseball bears an American imprint that has not faded in the process of its geographical spread. And much of baseball's character as a distinctive form of popular entertainment has been bound up with the political, demographic, economic, and cultural history of the United States. Still, to find the links between baseball and the country of its birth, one must move past the clichés that imply that "America's game" is intelligible only to U.S. audiences, that no other game played in the United States is as popular, or that the game's rules and structure express something in the exceptional character of the American people, U.S. democracy, or the nation's past. The proposal in 1954 by Jacques Barzun, a twentieth-century French émigré historian and cultural critic, that "whoever wants to know the heart and mind of America had better learn baseball, the rules, and reality of the game"[3] is significant less for its insight than for how often it is repeated, especially by European visitors and immigrants. This myth has been important to baseball culture for at least a century and a half. But that doesn't make it a reliable guide to the meaning of the game. Baseball has appealed to different segments of the U.S. population at specific moments in particular ways and for distinct reasons. Still, Americans could have played and watched other games, and in fact they always have. And even as Major League Baseball generates higher revenues than other sports leagues (largely because it features an unequaled 2,430 regular-season games annually), polls consistently show that more Americans follow football and basketball. It is reasonable to look for the meaning of baseball on American soil, of course, but it is unwise to confine the search there—or to expect discoveries throughout its borders.

The challenge of locating baseball goes beyond geography. Understanding the place of baseball today requires rummaging through its past. Baseball is a historically self-conscious sport, attuned to every detail of its own history, finding meaning in cumulative records, unprecedented feats, and storied traditions. Baseball fans live on more intimate terms with distant periods of their pastime's history than do equally passionate devotees of politics, theater, or even music. And despite conspicuous changes, both the recreational activity and the spectator sport that comprise baseball have exhibited remarkable continuity since the nineteenth century, notwithstanding widespread perceptions of change. Ironically, the familiar lament that today's game has been degraded beyond recognition over the span of a generation by the forces of commercialization is one of baseball's oldest and most persistent features. It took Jacques Barzun himself about two generations to recant. By the beginning of the current century, Barzun maintained that changes in the game had rendered his earlier position obsolete.[4] Such recanting reaffirms baseball's continuity rather than its transformation. At the very least, perennial complaints about how baseball has declined reflect and reinforce baseball's obsession with its own past. Thinking about baseball requires confronting its deep past and explaining its cultural meaning over time.

Nonetheless, this book doesn't proceed chronologically. Each chapter tracks a different feature, relationship, or tension in the sport's development since the nineteenth century. Each considers a site where baseball is crucially located: in cities and cityscapes; in the organizational forms of clubs and leagues; in the sacred scripture of rulebooks; in rites and rituals of manhood; along the routes of U.S. and Japanese imperial expansion; on shifting maps of race and ethnicity; at labor negotiations tables; in mass media; in the hearts and minds of partisan spectators; and amidst the lures and fantasies of recordkeeping and quantification. These are persistent themes throughout baseball's past, and thus they are among the subjects that fans are inevitably talking about, or taking for granted, when they talk about baseball. These are some of the places where baseball as we know it has come into being. And these are subjects that a history of baseball can, in turn, help us explore. Because contrary to Thomas Jefferson's pronouncement that "games played with a ball stamp no character on the mind,"[5] a ball sport that is also mass entertainment can be excellent to think with.

In probing the character and meaning of baseball entertainment, this book's itinerary roams beyond the field of play and frequently leaves the stadium altogether. But it does focus somewhat narrowly on the highest levels of competition, especially in North America. To be clear, this is not a history of Major League Baseball—or the Japanese or Caribbean leagues—at least not in the conventional sense. I do not catalogue teams, identify star players, assess record-breaking achievements, or narrate epochal events. But I do focus on the worlds that have formed around those leagues rather than on the many other venues and tiers of competition in which baseball is performed for spectators. By one reckoning, Major League Baseball accounts for just the tip of the iceberg of baseball entertainment. Most baseball players never set foot on a major league diamond, and more spectators, in the aggregate, attend live games at the minor league or high school levels than at the majors. But far fewer people attend those games remotely, revisit the results on the news, or in any other way *follow* the action out of the ballpark or beyond the confines of a particular contest. And whatever cultural significance baseball has acquired over the last two centuries is the result of it being followed, and not simply watched. Baseball's special place in the daily habits and ritual lives of masses of consumers is largely about the history of that following.

One question that an exploration of baseball's cultural history cannot adequately answer is *why* so many people in so many places care about the game enough to watch or follow it. Consumers in the modern world spend their time watching a range of spectacles and care about many current events. It would be a mistake to assume that what attracts some spectators to baseball is fundamentally different from what attracts them (or others) to soccer, soap operas, or electoral politics. Like various other attractions, baseball might offer its fans drama, vicarious competition, community, continuity with childhood, displays of athletic prowess, or simply an excuse for socializing with friends. The complex social and psychological dynamics that sustain this identity and engagement are not unique to baseball, but they are nonetheless crucial to the experience—and the business—of the sport. The book that follows doesn't expose the roots of the habits, passions, and compulsions that develop around modern entertainment. It seeks instead to illuminate one particular form of modern entertainment to which those habits, passions, and compulsions have been famously directed. Baseball is worth thinking about—and with—because tens of millions of people have paid attention to it. Why, exactly, they have paid attention is not easily answered. The nature, quality, and objects of that attention form the subject of this book.

2
Urban Settings

At the end of the nineteenth century, leading figures in organized baseball, by then a massively popular spectator sport in much of the United States, began promoting a spurious origin story that credited the invention of the game to a man named Abner Doubleday of Cooperstown, New York. The primary impetus for the Doubleday myth, which has not survived historical scrutiny, was an avowed desire to claim American paternity for a game that many recognized as a variant of the British game rounders. Locating the invention in a small town had the additional advantage of downplaying the fact that baseball's origins actually lay in the city.

Organized baseball's pastoral self-image is old, but the game's earliest players and spectators were city people. Baseball clubs were composed of urban artisans, clerks, and shopkeepers, and they played in city streets, parks, and amusement grounds in front of other city dwellers. These origins are unsurprising. Games can be played anywhere, of course, but spectator sports are typically urban pastimes. Like theatrical productions, athletic competitions require a dense population to provide audiences for repeated performances. In the longer term, spectator sports typically flourish in purpose-built arenas that only urban entertainment markets and leisure cultures can support. Sports also rely on publishing to cultivate and maintain a print audience, both to drum up interest in contests and to connect those contests meaningfully to one another. And printing, for much of its history, has been an urban occupation.

The crucial historical context for baseball's early history, and a necessary (though not sufficient) condition for its creation, was urbanization. At the beginning of the nineteenth century, the United States was an overwhelmingly rural nation—more so than any European nation at the time other than Poland. About 94 percent of the population lived in towns, villages, plantations, and farming communities of fewer than 2500 people. The cities that existed were relatively tiny. At a time when one million people lived in London and over half a million lived in Paris, the largest U.S. city in 1800 housed only 60,000. But over the ensuing century, a massive demographic change took place. Rural Americans moved to urban areas, and foreign arrivals settled disproportionately in cities. The growth of the biggest cities was especially spectacular. Already by 1860, New York was home to over 800,000 people, with neighboring Brooklyn (a separate municipality until 1898) holding an additional quarter of a million. In all, nine different U.S. cities, mostly in the Northeast and Midwest, had crossed the population threshold of 100,000 by the time of the U.S. Civil War. These were the milieus in which organized baseball took shape.

Baseball was not the only form of mass culture to thrive in big U.S. cities during the middle third of the century. Theater, black-face minstrelsy, P. T. Barnum's exhibitions, bareknuckle prizefighting, commercial sex, and even partisan politics and evangelical revivals all catered to an exploding market for information and entertainment in an anonymous world of transplants and strangers. So did the cheap daily newspapers and specialized weeklies that turned those activities into subjects of sustained popular interest. Some historians have suggested that the peculiar structure of baseball, with its emphasis on a perilous passage home through a circuit of bases governed by complex rules of safety and danger, appealed to displaced urbanites navigating unfamiliar cityscapes. Yet other, older sports with more traditional structures of competition and combat, such as horse racing and boxing, remained popular in U.S. cities as well. The point is not that the nineteenth-century American metropolis called baseball into being, but rather that only in such a setting—with media outlets, public transportation, commercial nightlife, and a growing class of wage-earners—could *any* modern spectator sport have developed.

The Cooperstown legend may have displaced baseball's origins to a village setting, but the choice of state was apt. Although the game was played in multiple cities, it was the two largest cities in New York State—the twin cities of New York and Brooklyn—that formed the new sport's epicenter. The first baseball clubs (early 1840s), the first known codification of the game's rules (1845), the first game played before paying spectators (1858), and the first purpose-built baseball stadium (1862) were all centered in or around those two cities. So were the first newspapers to cover baseball games. And it was the distinctive New York game (rather than the version played in New England, for example) whose rules and format came to be recognized and adopted elsewhere.

As the game exploded in popularity in the 1850s, boosters bestowed upon it the status of America's "national game," but that moniker's original meaning is easily misconstrued. It amounted to a claim that baseball was indigenous to the United States, not that it was played throughout the country; in much of the South, for example, it was practically unknown. By 1860, baseball was played in at least sixty-seven different U.S. cities, but it still bore the stamp of its metropolitan center: most of the nation's baseball clubs were in New York City or Brooklyn. Organized baseball was an urban affair, and cities with economic and transportation connections to New York were most likely to have clubs and spectators.

As the sport spread, teams, leagues, and competitions organized themselves along urban lines. The early New York and Brooklyn clubs took names that identified them with occupations or neighborhoods, but when teams proliferated elsewhere in the country and began touring, they typically represented entire cities. The players themselves might no longer hail from the metropolis under whose banner they played, but the club's "home field" was located there, as was its management. Teams might have additional names, but in the news coverage, those names were consistently paired in conjunction with a city: the Philadelphia Olympics, the Cincinnati Red Stockings, the Washington Nationals. This marked a departure from the pattern in other spectator sports in the mid-nineteenth century. Notable horse races pitted thoroughbreds from the South against those from the North. U.S. prizefighters more often represented their ethnic group, religion, or political party, rather than their city. But already by the 1860s, organized baseball reflected and reinforced urban identity and interurban competition.

Such competition has remained central to baseball as a spectator sport throughout its history. Baseball teams, especially at the professional level, continue to be named for the cities (rather than neighborhoods, counties, states, or regions) that the companies that own them call home, thereby establishing a model for other team sports in North America. At every professional level, U.S. baseball teams identify with a city, and they compete primarily with teams representing other cities. This has been the case consistently in the Major (National and American) Leagues since their inception. The handful of departures from this pattern are telling. In the second half of the twentieth century, as the U.S. population suburbanized and television and radio (which were less firmly identified with the city than the daily newspaper was) became more important, several new teams adopted state names. In this way, they hoped to claim multiple urban homelands or to justify playing in a suburban location (the Minnesota Twins and Texas Rangers exemplified both impulses). But the trend was short-lived. In the current century, two franchises—the Florida Marlins and the California Angels—switched or reverted to urban names, even though the Angels don't play in their eponymous city. Meanwhile, teams in Baltimore, San Francisco, Detroit, and Minneapolis have reinforced symbolic ties with their home cities by moving downtown or along urban waterfronts. Another partial exception took place early in the twentieth century in the Negro Leagues, where several clubs took names other than those of their hometowns, but Black baseball was even more thoroughly connected with specific cities, more intensely integrated into their civic life and leisure culture, and more likely to feature local players.

Outside the United States, professional teams identify with cities less emphatically. Japan's teams are generally known for the corporations that own them. Tokyo's Yakult Swallows and Yomiuri Giants are named for a beverage company and a media chain, respectively. The Hanshin Tigers, named for a railway company, are famously identified with Osaka and the Kansai region, but they have not featured the Osaka name since their early years, nor do the Orix Buffaloes, who unlike the Tigers play most of their home games in Osaka's city center. Until recently and for most of the history of Japanese professional baseball, Hiroshima was the only city identified in a team name (and perhaps not coincidentally the only one to benefit from municipal stadium financing). None of the six teams in the Dominican Professional Baseball League trumpets a city name, and the greatest historical rivalry is intraurban rather than interurban. Nonetheless, all of the professional baseball franchises in Japan and the Dominican Republic—as well as in Korea, Venezuela, Colombia, and wherever professional baseball has enjoyed mass spectatorship—are urban. Games are held in city venues and belong to the leisure culture of the cities they call home.

Professional baseball has, in turn, left its mark on big cities, especially in the United States. Large urban populations provide the mass audiences necessary for any sport to thrive commercially, and baseball entrepreneurs have built spectacular structures to accommodate crowds. Baseball fields themselves are relatively expansive, covering far more ground than boxing rings, tennis courts, bowling alleys, or indoor tracks, but baseball's growing impact on American urban space starting around the 1870s resulted from bigger stadiums with larger seating capacity, not from the dimensions of the outfield (which varied widely). Union Grounds in Brooklyn, the first enclosed baseball arena, held 1500 seated spectators when it opened in 1862. Boston's South End Grounds (opening in 1871)—a wooden structure generally cited as the first example of monumental architecture in the history of baseball—seated 5,000. By the 1890s, Exposition Park in Pittsburgh boasted over 10,000 seats. Two decades later, New York's Polo Grounds could fit more than 30,000. These capacious buildings were also increasingly conspicuous, featuring steel grandstands, elegant spires, and ornate façades. In an era when tall office buildings were only beginning to appear, few monumental suspension bridges dominated the skylines, and the grand civic architecture of the City Beautiful Movement was still in its blueprint stage, baseball spawned the most imposing edifices in the American cityscape.

Beyond their prominence, these stadiums were quintessentially urban spaces. Between 1870 and 1920, the venues where spectators gathered to watch baseball games were the places where the largest crowds converged in one spot on a regular basis. Only theater attracted more spectators, but theatrical entertainment was dispersed across a panoply of smaller houses. World's Fairs attracted bigger throngs, but once or twice in the lifetime of an individual city. Only an amusement park like Coney Island could compete. Baseball stadiums were paragons of modern urban life because, as the architectural critic Paul Goldberger has observed, they "created the greatest number of opportunities for shared social experience."[1]

In their early generations, the outdoor structures where urban masses watched professional baseball were situated in dense neighborhoods and connected to the rest of the city by horse-drawn railway or electric streetcar. The illustrious baseball venues of the early twentieth century, such as Shibe Park in Philadelphia, Forbes Field in Pittsburgh, and Ebbets Field in Brooklyn, were all located around mass transit. Brooklyn's team took its name—the Dodgers—from the fact that fans would dodge trolley cars to get to the game.

By the middle third of the twentieth century, however, a different approach to designing and developing baseball venues emerged. Cleveland Municipal Stadium (which opened in 1931) provided an early example. Located on the lakefront far from downtown, served by parkways and roads designed for automobiles, and built with significant public subsidy, this new type of sports venue initiated a trend in professional baseball in the United States that would predominate in the decades following the Second World War. Between 1960 and 1975, Major League Baseball teams moved into newly constructed multipurpose stadiums in Philadelphia, St. Louis, Cincinnati, Pittsburgh, Oakland, Kansas City, Houston, San Diego, Arlington (Texas), Flushing (New York), Bloomington (Minnesota), and Washington, D.C. Except for Busch Stadium in St. Louis, none stood downtown or at the center of a city. Metropolitan Stadium, where the Minnesota Twins played, was more typically situated—in a suburb that would become home to the Mall of America. Several of the venues took the name of the county, rather than the city, in which they were located. In most cases, baseball franchises shared these massive homes with teams from the National Football League, which by midcentury had become a major professional spectator sport and drew larger average crowds to their weekly games and shorter seasons than a typical baseball game attracted. Although the new arenas looked almost identical, they no longer sported an architectural style or projected an image unique to baseball. Some observers celebrated their coliseum-like grandeur, while others disparaged them as concrete donuts. Either way, their shared claims to modernity, rather than their distinctive features, marked baseball's place in the cityscape during the second half of the century (see Figure 2.1).

Figure 2.1 Shea Stadium, in Flushing, Queens, epitomized the trend in the 1960s toward publicly subsidized, car-friendly, symmetrical stadiums, located in more suburban settings and designed for both football and baseball. Upon the New York Mets' move from the old Polo Grounds to their new home in 1964, essayist Roger Angell remarked on the difference. "No longer snug in a shoebox, my companions and I were ants perched on the sloping lip of a vast, shiny soup plate, and we were lonelier than we liked." *Shea Stadium and parking fields, photograph, n.d. Department of Parks General Files, NYC Municipal Archives*

In a departure from earlier naming patterns, these venues were called *stadiums*. Of the twenty new homes into which Major League Baseball teams moved during the third quarter of the twentieth century, all but one bore the stadium moniker. (San Francisco's Candlestick Park was the sole exception; even Houston's famous Astrodome was originally christened Harris County Domed

Stadium.) In the late nineteenth century, purpose-built baseball structures went by *field* or *park*, suggestive of the welcome and salutary presence of nature. When U.S. cities were still growing explosively and when baseball was conspicuously located in their crowded centers, fans sat in buildings whose names (Exposition Park, Sportsman's Park, Ebbets Field) promised pastoral refuge. The first storied baseball venues in Japan, which opened in the 1920s and 1930s, followed a similar naming pattern. Koshien, outside of Osaka, and Korakuen, in Tokyo, share a suffix that means green space, garden, or park.

The name *park* was especially meaningful. Whereas field might also refer to the playing surface, park seemed more unambiguously to include the watching stands and all the other attractions beyond the ticketing gates, thereby linking baseball to other amusement sites. More obviously, calling baseball arenas parks in the late nineteenth century affiliated them with the urban park movement. New York's Central Park (where playing baseball was initially prohibited and remained off-limits to adults until the 1920s) opened in 1859, and cities across the nation quickly followed suit. These parks were massive engineering feats, intended by their designers and promoters to ameliorate urban ills (including disease and class conflict) by manufacturing pastoral landscapes within city limits. This ideal of *rus in urbe* (country in the city), which is central to baseball mythology, was neatly captured by the insistence that fans were sitting in a park—or a ballpark. Baseball is in fact the only sport in which games are staged in ballparks.

As teams migrated to coliseum-like structures and domed arenas, typically at the metropolitan periphery, the word "park" was dropped in favor of *stadium*. When baseball returned to downtown, the park names reappeared (Loan Depot Park, Oracle Park, and even a suburban stadium with a retractable roof christened The Ballpark at Arlington, Texas), perhaps as part of the nostalgia. Since 2000, almost every new venue in Major League Baseball has been a field or a park. These pastoral names subtly—and paradoxically—reaffirm a longstanding connection to the metropolis.

The only institutions other than cities that have proven capable of organizing baseball competition for spectators on a large scale have been schools and universities. Like cities, those institutions can corral audiences and generate communal loyalties among fans. But in the United States, college and high school baseball have always taken a back seat to the professional versions of the sport. Unlike basketball and American football, both of which first developed as collegiate sports, baseball professionalized early, and college baseball in North America has never really rivaled the major leagues, nor do high school or college games attract the audiences that basketball or football draw. In Japan, by contrast, the college game emerged before its professional counterpart, and the most storied and followed rivalries pitted university teams. But whether amateur or professional, whenever Japanese baseball games are staged as commercial entertainment, they have been urban. The earliest games that attracted mass spectatorship in Japan were between Tokyo universities. Summer Koshien, Japan's annual high school tournament which garners far more popular interest than any amateur baseball event in the United States, takes place just outside Osaka, a metropolis of millions.

Of course, plenty of baseball gets played in small towns and rural areas throughout the United States. As a recreational activity, as opposed to a spectator sport, baseball has especially thrived outside of cities, in part because it requires a larger playing surface than many other games (such as net sports), ideally a field that serves no other practical or recreational purpose. Because of the high price of urban real estate, setting aside a big plot of land for baseball can be prohibitively expensive and especially so when there is little prospect of attracting masses of paying spectators. Where land is cheaper, baseball fields proliferate relative to population, making it easier for more people to play. In the United States, baseball diamonds dot the rural landscape, and Little League teams typically form in small towns or suburbs. Significantly, Little League Baseball Inc. is headquartered in South Williamsport, Pennsylvania, a town with a four-digit population. The annual Little League World Series brings teams from across the globe to South Williamsport, where Major League Baseball also holds (since 2017) its Little League Classic, an official game between professional teams designed to promote and broadcast youth interest in the sport. The hoopla surrounding the Classic reinforces the notion that the stars of a big-city spectator sport come from the ranks of a game played primarily in the rural heartland.

Even more than the Little League Classic, the promotional event that best showcases the complex interplay of country and city in baseball mythology takes place in August in Dyersville, Iowa, where a baseball field was constructed for the movie set of the 1989 film *Field of Dreams*. Based on W. P. Kinsella's 1982 novel *Shoeless Joe*, the film features a writer-farmer protagonist who, prompted by a supernatural voice promising that "If you build it, he will come" (largely remembered or reinterpreted by movie viewers as "*they* will come"), builds a baseball diamond in his cornfield to which dead baseball greats return for a game. This in turn facilitates a game of catch between the main character and his deceased baseball-playing father with whom he had unresolved conflict. A box-office smash nominated for multiple awards, *Field of Dreams* remains one of the most popular and influential baseball movies of the last fifty years. Its appeal lies in its mobilization of familiar baseball tropes and clichés rather than in its construction of new ones. And the magical transformation of a cornfield in Iowa (a state long associated with both fiction writing and minor league baseball) into a baseball stadium was hardly a stretch. Baseball's fans and mythologists have always preferred to root the game in pastoral settings rather than crowded cities.

The ballpark built for *Field of Dreams* became an instant tourist attraction. A few hundred feet away, the property owners built a new field, configured for professional play, and modeled after a storied stadium in Chicago. Major League Baseball began staging the MLB at Field of Dreams game in 2021. Clad in retro uniforms from a century earlier, teams from New York and Chicago took the fabled field/set. Home runs sailed into rows of corn beyond the outfield fences, landing far from the big cities where this spectacle was produced. Reversing the game's traditional fantasy, Major League Baseball had managed to transplant *urbe in rus*—the city in the country.

3

Associations

Baseball is hardly unique among popular sports for featuring bands of players, but compared to many other team games, it is especially difficult to scale down. Basketball, for example, calls for five on a side, but it hasn't required much imagination to play a recognizable version of the game with teams of two or three—or just one. Even soccer, with its vast standard pitch and teams of eleven, can be easily contracted. And as with many team sports (including American football, field hockey, lacrosse, even cricket), the crucial point-scoring activities of basketball and soccer can be performed with only a couple of players. In baseball, scaling down is more challenging, since fielders must cover all four bases and patrol all areas where a ball can be fairly hit, and since points can't simply be scored by putting a ball in a net. To be sure, in the absence of sufficient space and numbers, people (especially children) have improvised over the years, playing variants such as stickball, wiffle ball, sandlot baseball, and *cuatro esquinas*, or practicing basic components of the sport at a batting cage or in a simple game of catch. But much as proper baseball occupies space, it also demands numbers.

From its inception, then, baseball has been a large-group activity. Men organized baseball clubs in U.S. cities to play a game that was hard to enact spontaneously and needed a substantial gathering. In crucial respects, these clubs resembled the many other organizations that men and women formed in towns and cities across the North and Midwest during the second quarter of the nineteenth century—fraternal orders, temperance societies, singing groups—that brought individuals together on a regular basis for activities requiring critical mass. Alexis de Tocqueville, the French observer of U.S. democracy in the 1830s, called these "voluntary associations," which he cited as central to American politics and culture. Baseball clubs developed within this world, and the fact that Major League Baseball's billion-dollar corporate entertainment franchises (unlike their counterparts in other U.S. team sports) are called *clubs* bears traces of that history.[1]

Clubs, as opposed to teams, are typically closed groups. Then and now, the things we call clubs (book clubs, chess clubs, country clubs) direct their activity and attention inward. Members of early baseball clubs, such as the New York Knickerbocker Club, shared and cultivated a love of the game, which they played with and against one another, not against outsiders. As clubs multiplied in New York, Brooklyn, and to a lesser extent other cities, they began inviting their counterparts to social events, featuring dinners, toasts, and match-games between each club's "first nine." The host and guest clubs would schedule the match and establish rules and stakes for what were still local affairs between two fraternities. No outside body or governing institution coordinated, regulated, or promoted competitions between clubs, though a nascent urban sporting press (which also covered theater, crime, and commercial sex) might report the outcomes of these club matches.

What baseball players and spectators did not have at midcentury was a *league*, which even more than the club is the core institution of modern baseball. Leagues are bounded realms of competition that make modern spectator sports meaningful over time. And whereas baseball clubs were adopting an established form used by reformers, tinkerers, musicians, and revelers, the baseball league was an innovation in the third quarter of the century. No comparable institution linked boxing matches or horse races at the time, nor did cricket or soccer leagues exist then in Europe. Having leagues does not distinguish professional baseball from other sports; instead, it marks one of subtler ways in which baseball's development in the nineteenth century laid foundations for other kinds of entertainment.

The emergence of the modern baseball league began in the late 1850s, when more than a dozen New York and Brooklyn clubs sought to bring order to their competitive landscape and promote public interest. At an 1857 convention, these clubs formed the National Association of Base Ball Players (NABBP), which was neither national in scope nor composed of players. It was also not a proper league in the modern sense, since it didn't create a bounded world of competition (clubs belonging to the NABBP played equally significant games against outside clubs) and initially eschewed awarding championships. Moreover, the Association only loosely regulated relations between clubs and players. But it did codify game rules for all member clubs, and in that sense it created something we might recognize as organized baseball.

As baseball grew in popularity as a spectator sport, competition between clubs (sometimes representing distant cities) became a potentially profitable entertainment enterprise, tempting club owners to do two things that violated Association principles: creating unofficial championships and paying outstanding players in the hopes of becoming champions. These two practices generated greater movement of players between clubs (*revolving*, as it was called), which underscored the fact that baseball clubs had drifted from their origins as social fraternities of men who shared neighborhoods, milieus, or occupations. Controversies over this development simmered, and in 1871 organized baseball splintered in two: an amateur association and a professional one.

The professional organization probably qualifies as baseball's inaugural league, arguably the first institution in modern sports history to create a durable circuit of competition for spectators to follow from year to year. As leagues go, it was relatively unstable. Clubs routinely failed in the middle of a season, and the association couldn't maintain a regular schedule. Still, the NABBP achieved several things central to what modern sports leagues do. Most significantly, it maintained undisputed control over the rules of play, set parameters for crowning a "Champion of the United States" (a distinction adopted from the boxing world), and asserted its interest in enforcing contracts between teams and their professional players, now redefined as employees. The league struggled with that last goal, as it did with inducing players and fans across the country to accept their designation of a champion, but the mere fact that there was now a corporate body other than a club producing a spectator sport for a commercial audience heralded the arrival of a modern era in baseball—and in sports more generally.

The relative impotence of baseball's first league becomes clearer in the shadow of a big change in 1876, when the new National League of Professional Base Ball Clubs replaced it. The change in name from *players* to *clubs* highlighted the power of team owners and a more rigid separation between management and employee, but the introduction of the word *league* was also significant. The National League, which has remained in continuous existence to this day, was a kind of cartel, pooling its resources and power to sell a single product—sustained competition. That product, rather than the clubs themselves or the talented individuals who played the game, was what leagues controlled, promoted, and commodified.

To consolidate this entertainment product, the National League (NL) scheduled all games and enacted rules for the conduct of business. Only cities with populations of at least 75,000 could be represented in the league, and no city could house more than one club. The league granted clubs exclusive rights to the services of their players and prohibited hiring any player dismissed by another club. Like many professional leagues that followed in its wake, in baseball and in other sports, the NL constituted a competitive structure and a centrally managed labor market. Plenty of independent baseball, both professional and amateur, would continue to take place beyond the league's patrolled borders, but in the new landscape created by this monopoly, significant challenges would take the form of rival leagues.

Three features of the NL opened paths to such challenges. First, the limit of one team per city meant that a new league (but not a new NL team) could compete for the significant fan demand in places like New York, Brooklyn, and Philadelphia. Second, the NL committed itself to maintaining a brand of baseball that upheld cultural values associated with middle-class Protestant respectability. Individual clubs subjected players to temperance oaths and bed checks, and the league held a firm line against alcohol sales and Sunday games. This created an opportunity for rival associations to cater to spectators whom the NL was deliberately neglecting. And finally, owners' agreement to depress pay and restrict player movement created an incentive for talented players to seek employment beyond the league's patrolled borders.

Early challengers to the National League pursued these opportunities. The American Association (AA), which was formed in 1881, awarded franchises to teams in big East Coast metropolises that had NL clubs, but it also established strongholds in cities along the Ohio and Mississippi rivers that had large immigrant populations. In St. Louis and Cincinnati, the Association appealed especially to German Americans, whose Sunday mores permitted commercial leisure and alcohol consumption. Dubbed the Beer and Whiskey League, the American Association also challenged the National League by offering cheaper admission and games on the one day every week when most baseball fans had off from work. Chris Von der Ahe, a beer seller who helped start the Association and owned the St. Louis Browns, personified the AA's rejection of NL ideals of respectability; Sportsman's Park in St. Louis featured a beer garden that extended onto the field of play and venues for bowling and shooting among the ballpark's various entertainment concessions. Perhaps not surprisingly, AA teams drew significant crowds, setting new attendance records for baseball.

Competition between the two leagues intensified in the 1880s. Each league modified the rules of play with an eye to keeping up with (or distinguishing itself from) its rival. A postseason championship between the NL's Providence Grays and the AA's New York Metropolitans in 1884 was the first such clash to be promoted as a "World's Series." On a couple of occasions, teams defected from one league to the other. After the 1891 season, however, the American Association disbanded, and its surviving teams were absorbed into the National League. By another measure, however, the Beer and Whiskey League prevailed. Lower admission prices, Sunday baseball, and beer sales became the norm in the NL.

Despite their rivalry, the two leagues conspired to limit player salaries and to honor each other's blacklists. This opened a lane for new leagues to recruit players as free agents paid at market rates. The first such rival, the Union Association, appeared in 1883, but suffered from lack of competitiveness (a dominant team from St. Louis won 83 percent of its games) and dissolved after a year. A more powerful challenge arose at the end of the decade in the form of the Players Association (led by Columbia Law School graduate John Montgomery Ward), whose cooperatively owned teams poached many of the other leagues' best players by sharing profits with them. But it too lasted only one season. By 1892, all rivals had abandoned the field, and the NL remained the only league that could claim to present top-tier professional baseball.

Throughout these early years of league baseball, various other associations of teams formed, mostly as regional theaters of competition (they took names like Northwestern, Western, and Eastern, as opposed to National, American, and Federal), without competing for players with the NL or claiming rival league status. But in 1900 one of these so-called minor circuits, the Western League, shed its regional garb and announced national ambitions. The renamed American League (AL) competed directly with the National League, not just for players, but also for fans, since most of its franchises played shared home cities with teams from the NL. The war between the leagues prompted extensive negotiations and formal overhaul of the sport. By the terms of a 1902 agreement, the two competing major leagues and a new National Association of Minor Leagues aligned their rulebooks, agreed to honor one another's contracts, and established a framework of U.S. organized baseball (anchored in something called the Major League Baseball Constitution). This framework would endure for the next century and initiate fifty years of extraordinary stability during which no franchise would enter or exit a major league and no team would relocate.

Starting in 1903, the NL and AL champions would compete annually in the Fall in a World Series. The term *World Series* certainly exuded provincialism and hubris, since baseball was already being played competitively in other countries, but it also reflected the fact that the names of the two leagues precluded calling the series American or National. Apart from this annual showdown, the AL and NL remained closed circuits, and clubs would compete only within their respective leagues. They could trade players across the divide, but those trades were subject to impediments and restrictions, especially before 1959. Each league would be governed separately, though after 1920 a Commissioner of Baseball was empowered to make decisions that would be binding on both. The two circuits possessed equal stature and colluded in selling the same entertainment product, but by many measures, the National and American Leagues were separate universes of competition for most of the twentieth century.

In the current century, that is no longer the case. At the dawn of the new millennium, Major League Baseball consolidated the two leagues under a single corporate entity. Regular-season interleague games began in 1997 and now account for over a quarter of each club's schedule. Trades between AL and NL teams are as common as those within league borders. And the significant rule difference that had divided the two leagues—for a half century beginning in 1973, the AL had allowed teams to designate a player who would hit but not take the field—was eliminated when MLB universally adopted the practice in 2020. The American and National Leagues are now better defined as conferences (like those in other major U.S team sports) than as leagues; Major League Baseball is itself the league.

Still, there have always been other leagues. Minor Leagues in North America, which account for the majority of professional baseball games, were once independent and self-contained, though ever since the Great Depression of the 1930s most have been affiliated with and subordinated to MLB, playing by its contract constraints and helping to develop its players. In other cases, a league has functioned more as a parallel universe than a satellite. Some of the most striking examples of this phenomenon are the seven American Negro Leagues that thrived between 1920 and 1950. These were weak leagues in the sense that they did not exercise effective control over player contracts or team business (the economics and geography of Negro baseball forced teams to play mostly beyond league borders in freestanding events known as barnstorming games), but they still had the power to determine which competitions counted. MLB has since 2020 recognized these leagues' official games as part of its own history, but it would be more historically accurate to see those entities as worlds apart, not only because they epitomized larger patterns of racial segregation in the United States, but because they sold to spectators a top-tier product of baseball play that could neither collude nor collide with the competition in the American or National League.

The same is true of the many national baseball leagues that have thrived outside the United States. A Cuban League formed in 1878, just two years after the National League. It recruited U.S. players (including many who were barred from the majors because of race) for its winter seasons and remained in operation until just after the 1959 Revolution. Japanese professional teams competed in a league beginning in 1936, but then they reorganized in 1950 under the U.S. occupation into a two-league structure based on the American model under the umbrella of Nippon Professional Baseball. (Because Japan's Central and Pacific League teams did not face each other during the regular season until 2005, they were genuinely distinct leagues, as the NL and AL had been.) Across the baseball map, in Korea's KBO (Korean Baseball Organization), LIDOM (Liga de Béisbol Profesional de la Republica Dominicana) in the Dominican Republic, the Australian Baseball League, and over a dozen others, the game is played in closed circuits of professional competition, though some leagues have more porous borders. The Czech Baseball Extraliga uses a relegation and promotion system (as in European soccer) in which clubs move from one league to another based on performance. Several of the major leagues in the Caribbean play short winter seasons culminating in a Caribbean Series (held since 1949) that crowns a single champion. But by most standards, these are still independent associations that sell the prospect and history of their internal competition to spectators and followers.

Amateur baseball leagues have also proliferated and endured, both in the United States and across the globe. Some of these leagues are national in scope, others are regional, and some affiliate with national umbrella organizations (like Little League Baseball or the NCAA). At every age level and every stage of schooling, teams playing baseball (and softball) have organized in leagues, typically to create procedures for determining championships, but also to permit recordkeeping and statistical continuity.

Baseball leagues are powerful institutions whose significance is commonly overlooked. Unlike divisions or conferences, which are subsets that segregate competition or map out paths for determining championships, leagues belong to nothing larger than themselves and typically answer to no higher authority. They maintain and define their own histories; nothing that takes place outside the boundaries of a sports league counts. This condition makes the league a suitable instrument for imagining or creating a fictional universe, which may explain why several classic baseball novels introduce leagues with tenuous claims to existence. Robert Coover's *The Universal Baseball Association, Inc., J. Henry Waugh,*

Prop. (1968) fleshes out a baseball league, complete with psychologically complex players and managers and a storied and statistically detailed past, which is entirely the fantastic creation of an accountant rolling dice at his kitchen table. Philip Roth's *The Great American Novel* (1973) conjures the opposite specter: a thriving major baseball league that the sporting establishment and the U.S. government have conspired to erase from history. W. P. Kinsella's *The Iowa Baseball Confederacy* (1986) features a plotline that combines those scenarios. In Kinsella's story, a man devotes his life to proving the existence of a defunct minor league, but a league trapped inside his head, for which there is no historical evidence. Leagues, like fiction, invite spectators into framed worlds with peculiar rules about what really happened.

4

The Rule of Law

On April 6, 1973, Ron Blomberg of the New York Yankees came to bat against the Boston Red Sox as the first designated hitter in the regular-season history of Major League Baseball. Breaking from traditions as old as the organized sport, a new rule exclusive to the American League (AL) allowed a batter to play the entire game without ever taking the field. For the next fifty years, the American and National Leagues would play by different rules, highlighting in the process the power of leagues to define and redefine the parameters of legitimate play in a modern spectator sport.

Other leagues—both professional and amateur, in multiple countries—began following the AL's example, allowing teams to spare their pitchers from having to hit by substituting batters in their place. Half a century after its introduction, the designated hitter is broadly accepted as a basic feature of baseball; only in Japan's Pacific League are pitchers still required to take their turn at bat. But for several years after Blomberg's 1973 appearance, the rule spawned controversy. Motivated by a desire to boost scoring, justified by the argument that pitchers (like goalkeepers in soccer or placekickers in American football) possess a specialized talent that does not typically correlate with the sport's other skills, and ultimately supported by unions and agents seeking to preserve or prolong career opportunities for hitters with poor or declining fielding proficiency, the designated hitter rule had to overcome charges of heresy. Critics asked whether a game in which players were allowed to bat but not take the field was still baseball.

Such controversies are understandable. Sports are defined by their rules, and sports played under sufficiently different regulatory regimes can plausibly be regarded as different sports altogether. Much of why modern fans and sportswriters don't recognize nineteenth-century baseball as part of the game's proper history is a matter of rule difference. When New York's Knickerbocker Club codified their rules of play in 1845, often considered a foundational moment in baseball history, the game included numerous features that would render it illegible to spectators across the world today. Games would end when one team scored twenty-one runs, bases were positioned at distances shorter than 90 feet, and pitchers were enjoined to toss the ball underhanded. All these differences cut to the heart of what many fans now assume defines the sport.

Some alien features of baseball as prescribed by the Knickerbocker code disappeared as the New York game achieved broader popularity. But others lingered. A batted ball caught after a bounce produced an out until 1865; pitching overhanded remained illegal through 1883; the allotment of three strikes and four balls took hold only in 1889; and the current distance between pitcher and batter (which baseball mythologists cite as key to the game's perfection) arrived in 1893. Even in the twentieth century, after the agreement between the two major U.S. leagues inaugurated baseball's modern era, the rulebook remained subject to frequent alteration regarding things as fundamental as the material composition of the ball, the conditions of an automatic home run, the minimum size of an outfield, the height of the pitcher's mound, and the definition of a strike zone relative to a batter's body. The designated hitter rule, in other words, stood in a long tradition of legal innovations. Outside the United States, professional leagues have modified or implemented rules as well. In Japan, Korea, and Taiwan, for example, a game can end in a draw if the score remains tied after three extra innings, and Japanese games have a time limit of 3.5 hours.

Debates as to whether rule changes and variations transform baseball's essential character beg the question of what one takes that essence to be. That question is muddied in turn by the different things fans and critics might be trying to explain when they call a rule fundamental. Is the issue what makes baseball appealing? What makes baseball distinctive among sports? Or what gives baseball continuous meaning over time? Among the welter of rule modifications that have been introduced since the 1840s, none seems to be an obvious candidate to account for the sport's appeal or its distinction. Taken together, however, these differences break the continuity between early baseball and today's game. When bases were separated by shorter distances, when a ball hit to foul territory didn't count as a strike against the batter, or when (as was the case in the major leagues in 1887) a batter was allowed four instead of three strikes, was it the same game we watch now?

Perhaps the strongest argument that rule changes fundamentally altered the sport lies in the case of pitching. When the aging poet Walt Whitman, who decades earlier had been a baseball reporter, learned in 1889 that "the fellow who pitches the ball aims to pitch it in such a way that the batter can't hit it," Whitman pronounced the change "everything that is damnable."[1] However one valued it, the shift was dramatic. When pitchers were required to enable rather than to thwart hitting (like a coach or parent in a children's game, lobbing the ball softly and neutrally toward the plate), the crucial contest pitted hitters against fielders, not hitters against pitchers. From the 1880s on, by contrast, the confrontation between batter and pitcher has been the principal focus of tension in the game, and subsequent legal changes (from mound distance to ball density to strike zone) have mostly sought to regulate the balance in that confrontation.

This tangled history of regulations makes it hard to use the rulebook to pinpoint the essence of organized baseball—or to figure out when baseball's proper history began. But if there was something foundational in the Knickerbockers' 1845 code, it lay in the simple act of recording rules. Baseball is hardly the only sport to live under the rule of law—having a rulebook is arguably among the prerequisites for being a modern spectator sport—but it was a model. Baseball fans recognize in the Knickerbocker code not so much its particular rules of play (though many have proven remarkably enduring), but rather its formality, precision, and detail. Even more recognizably modern is the *Constitution and Playing Rules of the National League of Professional Base Ball Clubs*, first published by A. G. Spalding and Brother in 1877. Spalding's rulebook, which would be revised annually, is the oldest such publication in the history of American team sports, and it was with this text in hand that Hiraoka Hiroshi spread the gospel of baseball in Japan in the 1870s.

Though frequently amended and renewed, *Official Baseball Rules* remains sacred scripture for professional play throughout North America. Unlike the MLB Constitution, a separate document that governs business operations, disciplinary practices, labor relations, revenue sharing, and league competition, the rulebook concerns itself with what happens on the field of play; therefore, it can be applied to baseball settings over which the MLB has no formal jurisdiction. It is a massive tome (now accessed mostly electronically), filling around two hundred pages (depending on edition and format), with prescriptions at a level of such intricate detail that even experienced players, coaches, and commentators might consult it to resolve uncertainty or dispute. It ranges widely, articulating the "objectives of the game," prescribing field layout, choreographing the exchange of lineup cards, and defining—and castigating—unsportsmanlike conduct. Rule 6.02(c)(9) states: "To pitch at a batter's head is unsportsmanlike and highly dangerous. It should be—and is—condemned by everybody." Detailed rules govern right-of-way conflicts between fielders and runners, spectator interference, weather and field conditions, and ambidextrous pitchers.[2]

Significantly, certain matters go unmentioned in the rulebook. Beyond its purview lie norms of conduct known as "unwritten rules," most of which are related to manly honor. These rules include taboos against excessive displays of self-admiration and protocols of retaliation for getting hit by a pitched ball. The notorious ban on Black players in U.S. major leagues, long referred to as a "Gentleman's Agreement," also belonged to this oral honor code. As in many honor cultures, uncodified norms and extralegal remedies govern matters of personal honor. But the proportion of rules that remain unwritten is strikingly small.

Perhaps the most intriguing feature of the *Official Baseball Rules* is its commitment to legislating things that fall under the category of statistics. What counts as a win, a loss, or a shutout for the pitcher? Under what circumstances does a batter receive credit for batting in a run? What determines whether a ball that eludes the grasp of the catcher gets called a wild pitch (charged to the pitcher) or a passed ball (charged to the catcher)? Unlike rules about fair and foul balls or legal and illegal equipment, none of these questions bears on the outcome of a game. Instead, they matter only for the historical record.

The lumping together of game rules and statistical recordkeeping as things requiring official governance was anticipated by a peculiar feature of the Knickerbocker code. The second Knickerbocker rule called for the appointment of a single "Umpire, who shall keep the game in a book provided for that purpose, and note all violations of the By-Laws and Rules during the time of exercise." The umpire's now-familiar task of adjudicating "disputes and differences relative to the game" was thus combined with that of being the game's official chronicler. Keeping track of the score is of course necessary for conducting the game—especially when games ended only once a team had scored twenty-one runs, but also in the modern nine-inning structure. But the umpire was tasked with recordkeeping more generally.[3] Organized baseball would separate the roles of umpire, whose decisions (about balls and strikes, runs and outs, fair and foul) affect the outcome, and those of official scorer, whose decisions (about hits and errors, pitcher wins, and pitcher losses) do not. Still, the rulebook covers both sets of decisions. And both kinds of regulation form the legal regime under which players, management, reporters, and fans all live.

Professional baseball leagues beyond the United States also share this legal culture. The rules of play in Japan differ in a few particulars, as do the rules of recordkeeping. A run scored because of a fielding miscue, for example, has the official legal status of an "unearned run" in both countries, which means that it does not count against the record of the pitcher who surrendered it. (This has absolutely zero significance for the game score.) But in the American game, that run can become retroactively "earned" if a subsequent hit would have caused the runner to score even without the earlier error. This is not the case in Japan. The subtle difference in the rules governing unearned runs is far less striking than the fact that both systems of organized baseball place such questions in the domain of the official rulebook.

Appropriately, the preamble to the *Official Baseball Rules* declares faith in the rule of law. After affirming baseball's status as "the National Game of the United States" and celebrating its growing appeal as a global sport "played in more than 100 countries," the rulebook cautions that this popularity "will grow only so long as its players, managers, coaches, umpires and administrative officers respect the discipline of its code of rules."[4] The discipline invoked is not simply obedience and self-control; it is the discipline of consulting and navigating legal systems.

Whereas Major League Baseball has modeled a relationship to legal order that characterizes organized baseball generally, its own legal system has an unusual feature. Since 1920, MLB has empowered a powerful executive, called a Commissioner, whose word is law. This executive power has been designed primarily to regulate business and labor relations rather than the rules of play, but the commissioner's supremacy theoretically trumps that of the rulebook. The office originated in 1920, in the wake of the infamous scandal the prior year, when members of the Chicago White Sox took bribes from gamblers to fix the result of the World Series. Seeking to restore fan confidence in the sport's integrity, league owners brought in federal judge Kenesaw Mountain Landis and vested him with unlimited authority over everyone employed by any team. Landis wielded this authority with little restraint during his twenty-four years in office, and his successors more or less followed his example. Most famously, commissioners continued to enforce (unilaterally) the lifetime ban against Pete Rose, a superstar from the 1970s and 1980s who was only reinstated after his death in 2024, for betting on baseball.

The role of gambling in shifting MLB's legal system from one dominated by scripture to one dominated (at least in principle) by a strongman is notable. Codifying rules and formalizing the procedures for determining the outcome of a game make a sport suitable for wagers in the first place, which in turn helps sustain fan interest. Games without formal and broadly legible rules are harder to bet on, but so are games where participants are suspected of manipulating the outcome to serve a wagering interest. The specter of players fixing a World Series threatened the integrity of the wager as well as the integrity of league competition. Empowering a commissioner was designed to keep gambling interests from corrupting the game, but it also had the effect of reassuring gamblers that the rules of baseball would be sufficient to make baseball the subject of a fair bet.

Under the leadership of its current commissioner, Major League Baseball has been an active legislator. New rules in recent years have introduced instant replay reviews, restricted defensive positioning, spread the designated hitter to the National League, and altered the frequency with which teams play one another. Several changes have been designed to speed up the game (by regulating pitcher replacements and limiting the time between pitches) or to shorten the game (the radical innovation of spotting each team a runner on second base, charmingly dubbed the "Manfred man" in dubious homage to Commissioner Rob Manfred, during extra-inning play). Other changes pursue the perennial goal of increasing offense, though that goal conflicts with that of speeding up the game. Yet others respond to the perception, boosted by newer technologies of video capture, that umpire judgments are flawed. All of these changes, like many that preceded it, are aimed at enhancing the appeal of baseball as commercial entertainment, and most of these changes have parallels in other sports across the world. None of the new rules alters the basic legal character of baseball, which is really about the relentlessness and omnipresence of law itself.

5

Manhood

In the most frequently quoted line from Penny Marshall's hit movie *A League of Their Own* (1992), Tom Hanks (as Jimmy Duggan) proclaims, almost in a plaintive whine, that "there's no crying in baseball." As a description of the sport, the line is patently false. A game over which neither players nor fans can be moved to tears by frustration, joy, disappointment, or crushed hope would never attract so much attention or generate so much money. But as an attempt to lay down norms of conduct, Duggan's iconic line, delivered to women playing professional baseball, stands in a grand tradition.

From its earliest history as an organized sport, baseball has struggled to assert its manhood. This is a common predicament in modern sports. But baseball's claims to manliness assumed special urgency in nineteenth-century America because of the game's history, the contemporary sporting scene, and broader debates over masculinity.

At the time of baseball's emergence in the United States, claiming manhood was about more than just affirming masculinity. It meant distinguishing oneself from at least of one of four different identities: woman, child, slave, and beast. The last contrast did not figure in the game's development, nor was baseball commonly accused of being a game fit for slaves—at least not explicitly. Cultural historian Kenneth Greenberg has argued that baseball's lack of popularity in the antebellum South (which might also be explained by the region's low rate of urbanization) reflected a clash between a southern culture of honor and a sport that rewarded deception, eluding capture, and other activities that slaveholders identified with the people they held as chattel.[1]

Baseball also encountered resistance in other cultural contexts where subterfuge and cunning were contrasted with manhood—not because baseball was feminine, but because it was less honorable. Inazo Nitobe, later Japan's representative to the League of Nations, disparaged baseball in 1911 as a sport of pickpockets, fit for Americans. "To play baseball, you must be able to deceive the opposing team and lead them into a trap. You must always sharpen your senses so that you will never miss the chance to steal a base." Real men, Nitobe maintained, would prefer the British game of rugby.[2]

Baseball's early promoters and practitioners worried less about being mistaken for slaves or thieves and more about charges of boyishness. Whenever adults play games that don't involve direct physical combat—and take seriously their outcomes—they risk accusations of childishness. But baseball faced a particular challenge because of its evident descent from the English game of rounders, and disavowing that genealogy was not merely a point of national pride. Rounders, as an 1860 baseball publication insisted, was a children's game "designed only for relaxations during the intervals between study in school." It was "entirely devoid of the manly features" of baseball, which "requires…muscular strength, readiness of hand, and many other faculties of mind and body that mark a man of nerve." This obsession with protecting the manly art of baseball from juvenile impulses and influences surfaced repeatedly in the sport's formative years. Even the pivotal debate in the 1850s and 1860s about the "fly rule" seemed to hinge on this question. Those who wished to abandon the established norm of counting a batted ball caught after a single bounce as an out attacked what they called a "boy's rule." Fielding a ball after a bounce was a "boys' play," wrote one sports paper in 1859. If baseball was to be a sport for grown men, reformers argued, the rules needed to raise the difficulty of fielding.[3]

Boyishness and boyhood were not eliminated from baseball, but they were held at a distance. Boys entered the sport as a rite of gradual passage into manhood. Although boys would play informal versions of the game in city streets and rural sandlots, the organized spectator sport of baseball remained adult-dominated throughout the nineteenth century, both in the United States and abroad. High school baseball competition attracted significant fan interest in Japan but not before the 1890s; it spread even later in North America. Not until the 1930s would children's leagues organize in the United States. Adults (especially fathers) would initiate boys (especially sons) into the pleasures of the game, yet the prototype of a baseball player would remain a physically mature and legally independent man.

Manhood in nineteenth-century America was about masculinity, of course, not just adulthood, and the most carefully monitored boundaries of manhood delimited gender, not age. Boys might prepare themselves for manhood, but girls and women stood definitively removed from its privileges. Both girls and women haunted and threatened baseball's claims to masculinity, in part because English girls had long played rounders and similar games. This phenomenon is famously attested in Jane Austen's 1817 novel *Northanger Abbey*, where the game is in fact called "base ball" rather than rounders. American women played baseball in numerous settings and venues during the nineteenth century, in baseball clubs at women's colleges (Vassar's baseball club predated the National League), for example, and on barnstorming teams that played individual games beyond the domain of organized league baseball (Figure 5.1).

In the early decades, codes of masculinity required keeping women at the margins of the playing field, but they did not exclude them altogether. For many of the game's promoters and players, baseball represented a particular model of masculinity that was gaining traction in the nineteenth century. American baseball evangelists championed a gentler, less martial masculine ideal that emphasized discipline and self-control rather than combat. This

Figure 5.1 Although baseball clubs flourished in women's colleges in the nineteenth century, they generally did not play in front of crowds. Before that taboo settled in, however, the novelty of an all-women's game could attract favorable, if somewhat sensational, notice. According to a New York City newspaper in 1868, the members of this women's club from upstate, having "already arrived at a credible degree of proficiency . . . played a public game in the town of Peterboro, as may well be supposed, before a multitude of spectators." *"The Last Illustration of Women's Rights—A Femele [sic] Base-Ball Club at Peterboro, N.Y." The Days' Doings, October 3, 1868.* American Antiquarian Society (AAS), Historical Periodicals Collection: Series 5.

ideal, linked to middle-class respectability and trumpeted by various social reform causes, recommended baseball to its boosters over the popular sport of prizefighting, whose claims to being a "manly art" rested more overtly on violence, domination, individual glory, and bodily display.[4]

The loudest voice in this culture war over sports and masculinity belonged to Henry Chadwick, often hailed as one of baseball's founding fathers. Chadwick, the pioneering English-born sports-writer who established the game's early preoccupation with statistics and recordkeeping, saw baseball as a social reform cause. The game, in his words, provided "moral recreation" for respectable males, "a remedy for the many evils resulting from the immoral associations [that] boys and young men of our cities are apt to become connected with." When Chadwick and like-minded Protestant, middle-class reformers lamented that "the saloon and brothel are the evils of the base ball world at the present day," they meant not only that those two vices were responsible for inferior performance on the field, but also that those institutions were the sport's ideological enemies.[5] Baseball promised a spectacle and a social setting that could compete with the masculinist spaces and activities traditionally associated with sporting competition.

The presence of respectable women was crucial to that promise. The reformist model of manhood was heterosocial, in part because reformers like Chadwick saw women as salutary moral influences on men. As historian Warren Goldstein has argued, midcentury clubs and promoters hoped to draw fans "by the legitimacy that only women could confer on the game," because only women could "help men control themselves on the ballfield."[6] Whereas other sports and games offered men the opportunity to demonstrate prowess free of the domesticating influence and judgment of women, baseball (like the new forms of American theater that were emerging in this period) invited female spectatorship in order to provide an alternative.

Women were thus legitimate, even necessary, baseball fans from the sport's genesis. Although men predominated in crowded stands and stadiums, women were generally a welcome presence. But on the most prominent baseball fields, women were far scarcer. Women continued to play baseball, but mostly not in front of paying spectators, with a few notable exceptions. In 1883, for example, the all-female (and all-Black) Dolly Vardens of Chester, Pennsylvania, became the first professional women's baseball team on record. Other semiprofessional teams were mixed-gender, such as the barnstorming squads for which professional male superstars Rogers Hornsby and Smoky Joe Wood both played at one point. Professional league baseball remained off limits to women, though the prospect of women's play attracted little comment through much of the nineteenth century.[7]

Around 1890, the situation changed. Amidst rising anxieties about masculinity (exemplified by the complaints of Theodore Roosevelt about the feminization of American men), cultural critics turned their attention to the proper function of sports as masculinizing projects. Several new team sports appeared on the U.S. landscape at this moment, and all of them were defined around gender. First was American football, which emerged in the last quarter of the century as a college sport and gained prominence in the 1890s as a way to develop traditional martial manhood. At the same time, basketball was invented and immediately identified as an indoor sport suitable for both men and women. And finally, indoor baseball was invented and developed in the late 1880s by Midwestern men seeking to play some version of baseball on cold winter days. Indoor baseball competed (unsuccessfully, for the most part) with basketball for gymnasium space, moved outdoors, and was quickly deemed appropriate for girls and women. By the 1920s, it had standardized rules, equipment, and (diminished) field dimensions—all premised on making the game simpler and safer—and it was christened "softball." The ball was not particularly soft, but the game was designed to be.

With football claiming to make manlier men and softball offering a segregated space for girls and women to play, organized baseball sought to make it explicit as possible that it was for males only. In the canonical statement of major league ideology, Albert Spalding's *America's National Game* (1911) defined baseball's essential characteristics. Spalding, the former player and manager who had helped establish the National League while establishing himself as a sporting goods magnate, was baseball's most prominent promoter during the four decades before the First World War.

The sport he was promoting in 1911 had entered a golden age of nationwide prestige and popularity, and he took great pains to proclaim its preeminent masculinity. "Cricket is a gentle pastime," he observed, while "Base Ball Is War!" And whereas women might easily play cricket—"though they seldom do," he allowed, somewhat inaccurately—"neither our wives, our sisters, our daughters, nor our sweethearts may play Base Ball on the field." Unlike tennis, basketball, and golf, Spalding maintained, "Base Ball is too strenuous for womankind."[8]

In the same breath, however, Spalding celebrated female spectatorship. A woman has no place on the field, but "she may take part in grandstands." Spalding noted approvingly the rising number of women of all ages who followed the game knowledgeably. He hailed the woman who applauds "the brilliant play, with waving kerchief" and, as "loyal partisan of the home team," chides the umpire and tries to intimidate the other team's pitcher.

Spalding's description bore a striking resemblance to an earlier, far more enduring, tribute to women's baseball fandom. Just three years prior, a song written by men for the vaudeville stage introduced Katie Casey to American popular culture. Katie (variants of the song call her "Kitty Casey" or the equally Irish "Nelly Kelly") was "baseball mad / Had the fever and had it bad." She attended games regularly, knew all the players' names, "told the umpire he was wrong," and led the crowd in cheering for the home team. When her suitor offered to take her to the theater (or in some versions, to an amusement park), she demurred, instructing him instead: "Take me out to the ballgame / Take me out with the crowd / Buy me some peanuts and Cracker Jack / I don't care if I never get back."[9] The song's chorus would eventually become baseball's unofficial anthem; it is chanted ritually in professional games across North America and even in Japan, but few fans today recognize its origins as a woman's plea (scripted by men) for a particular kind of date. The 1908 song, like Spalding's manifesto, cultivated and canonized the woman in the stands.

Katie Casey has many descendants in American popular culture. From Bernard Malamud's 1952 novel *The Natural* to Ron Shelton's hit romantic comedy *Bull Durham* (1988) and well beyond, knowledgeable or obsessive female baseball fans are stock characters. Significantly, their love of the game is generally embedded in (or triangulated with) a heterosexual romantic interest, much as it is in "Take Me Out to the Ballgame." But that interest does not complicate these characters' devotion to the game. A competing tradition disparages female fan engagement with baseball as shallow, uninformed, fickle, or discredited by erotic motivations. This could include the adoring fan-girl (a stereotype more common in the world of popular music), who might be knowledgeable about the individual identities and accomplishments of particular players without truly understanding the game (much as teenage girls who worshiped Elvis and the Beatles were depreciated as music critics). Media coverage of Japanese baseball often emphasizes this type of fan.

More commonly, the professed interests of girls and women in baseball have been dismissed as insincere or unfounded, rather than being seen as inappropriately passionate. Canadian author Stacey May Fowles, citing her experiences as fan and sportswriter, has described these persistent stereotypes incisively, and any number of twentieth-century examples could reinforce her point. A 1962 *Sports Illustrated* profile of Joan Whitney Payson, the original majority owner of the New York Mets, included the following observation: "Women go to baseball games with their men rather than stay home alone and some even follow the results in the press so they can appear interested. But few really enjoy the game for its own sake."[10] It is worth noting that all stereotypes of female fandom, whether deep or shallow, emphasize the masculinity of the performers and the heteroerotic foundations of a woman's relationship to the game. Baseball is not unique among modern sports in this regard, but its longstanding need to include women at the margins makes it an especially illuminating case study.

Even as baseball officials and promoters sought to restrict and regulate the place of women, girls and women have forged relationships to the sport. First and foremost, they have formed teams and leagues and have played before paying spectators. The All-American Girls Baseball League featured in *A League of Their Own*, which began during the Second World War and survived for twenty years (longer than most professional baseball leagues in history), is the most prominent example, but hardly the only one. Individual women also played on predominantly male minor league teams in the 1930s, and an all-female team called the Sun Sox sought entry (unsuccessfully) into the Florida State League (Class A minors) in the 1980s. In recent decades, professional women's leagues have emerged in other countries as well, notably in East Asia and Cuba, enabling world cups and other international competitions.

Over the last half century, U.S. civil rights politics and feminist movements in multiple nations have shattered some of the barriers that have obstructed or confined girls' and women's participation in the spectator sport of baseball. In the United States, the 1964 federal Civil Rights Act, Title IX of the 1972 Education Amendments, and judicial applications of the equal protection clauses of federal and state constitutions forced schools, colleges, and youth organizations to include girls and women in their sports programs on equal terms. This process played out somewhat differently in baseball, however, both because softball existed as a segregated option for girls and because Little League Baseball mounted a concerted effort to defend its commitment, inscribed in its 1964 charter, to inculcating "citizenship, sportsmanship, and manhood." As one league official argued, baseball (presumably distinct from the other sports that the government was desegregating at the time) had been broadly accepted "as a male prerogative of some sort." But the courts began to reject these arguments, interpreting "manhood" as adulthood, and Congress amended the charter to strike the contentious word. In 1974, U.S. girls had secured the legal right to play.[11]

Yet few did. Little League quickly established a softball division, and girls flocked there instead. Despite the occasional flash of a superstar adolescent like Mo'ne Davis, who graced the cover of *Sports Illustrated* in 2014 after becoming the first girl to pitch a shutout in the Little League World Series, North American youth baseball remains almost entirely male. Davis herself went on to play college softball. In Japan, by contrast, girls have more opportunities to play baseball before spectators, both because Japanese institutions haven't been as invested in segregating baseball and softball and because high school baseball is a bigger spectator sport more generally.

Major League Baseball no longer appears to be invested in gender restriction as a means of preserving the game's manhood. With stiff competition for athletic talent and consumer attention from football, basketball, soccer, and extreme individual sports, MLB sees the gender line as an impediment to market access. Teams have sought (sometimes in awkward and demeaning ways) to attract women to ballparks, while also expanding the presence of women in and around the field of play. This century has seen pioneering appearances of women in professional baseball—as coaches, umpires, managers, corporate executives, and stadium announcers. Women are just now beginning to play on previously all-male college teams. It may be a while before a woman cracks a major league roster or that of professional men's teams in East Asia or the Caribbean. But the spectacle of more women on fields and in dugouts has broken down the division between a man's stage and a heterosocial gallery, which has long structured baseball as commercial entertainment.

Perhaps the most interesting blurring of that divide has been in the new prominence of women sportscasters, most often as post-game interviewers, but sometimes as color commentators or play-by-play announcers. In these roles, women appear both as exemplary spectators and as integral features of the performance in the most popular formats of baseball entertainment.

Male fans, at least in the United States, have been slow to adjust. When the former softball star Jessica Mendoza became the first woman to call (narrate) a nationally televised big-league baseball game in 2015, many viewers complained to the network that her presence and voice were somehow wrong. ("It killed it for me, sorry," one wrote.) Others questioned her qualifications by citing the irrelevance or inadequacy of her softball experience. One angry spectator, unironically invoking the sexism toward women newscasters parodied in the 2004 movie *Anchorman*, chimed in: "Yes tell us Tits McGhee when you're up there hitting the softball you see a lot of 95 mile an hour cutters?"[12] Although viewers may grow accustomed to the sound of a woman calling a home run, severing the link between baseball and manhood will require overcoming more than just habit. It entails a critical retreat from one of the sport's longest crusades.

6

Empires

In the middle of the nineteenth century, baseball as we know it was an exclusively American spectator sport, popular only in the nation's urban Northeast and centered in New York and Brooklyn. In the twenty-first century, baseball is played in more than one hundred countries and followed remotely in dozens of others. Professional baseball leagues entertain live spectators in Karachi, Caracas, Canberra, and countless locales far from New York City. Major League Baseball, whose players hail from over fifty different nations and territories, has staged official games in Mexico, Japan, Australia, South Korea, Great Britain, and France. Twenty-three national teams have qualified for an international championship, the World Baseball Classic, modeled after soccer's World Cup.

Still, baseball's global reach remains limited in significant ways. Whole portions of the world remain largely indifferent to the sport: the former Soviet Union, for example, as well as Scandinavia, Southeast Asia, much of the Mediterranean world, and almost every place colonized by Great Britain (and introduced to soccer) in the nineteenth century. U.S. baseball leagues continue to dominate and direct the game's spread abroad—from a headquarters in New York no less. Moreover, the places where baseball is most popular bear the heavy stamp of U.S. imperial influence. "Baseball follows the flag," Albert Spalding announced proudly in his 1911 paean to "America's National Game," citing the sport's capacity to spread American civilization and manhood to newly acquired colonial possessions in the Philippines, Puerto Rico, and Hawaii.

But like other attempts to understand baseball as a uniquely American pastime, Spalding's account of the sport's imperial expansion is a misleading guide to its global history. Baseball did play its part in American imperialism, especially after 1898, when the United States claimed possession of Puerto Rico, Guam, the Philippines, and the Hawaiian Islands. Accordingly, the earliest recorded baseball games in such places as Manila, Herschel Island (Alaska), and Agana all took place in the wake of imperial expansion, which was also when the major leagues consolidated their supreme position in the landscape of American commercial entertainment. But other countries have exported baseball as well. It makes more sense to read the current map of baseball as the handiwork of three different sports empires: the United States, Cuba, and Japan.

Cuba's history as an international baseball hub is distinctive. When baseball arrived on the island in the 1860s, just as the sport was taking off on the American mainland, Cuba was a Spanish colony with close ties to the United States through travel, migration, trade, and political sympathy. Cuba's baseball pioneers had learned the game while studying or traveling in American cities, and they introduced it upon their return home. By 1879, long before the Spanish-American War ended Spanish rule and brought Cuba under U.S. hegemony, the island boasted a professional baseball league. In the 1880s, sports publications with names like *El Pitcher* and *El Score* proliferated, advertising games played in Cuba and in North America. Opposition to the Spanish regime heightened the sport's appeal as an alternative to the soccer favored by colonial officials, who in turn saw the new American import as a political threat and closely monitored baseball activities.

Anticolonial politics was only a small part of the context for the growth of Cuban baseball. Cuban cities were connected to other Caribbean ports and to metropolitan areas across the United States through the exchange of people, goods, and information. Cuban baseball players and news traveled along that circuit, spreading the game to cities in Puerto Rico and the Dominican Republic and bringing within its orbit North American players and fans from Jacksonville to San Francisco. From a U.S. perspective, Cuban baseball offered two attractions. One was its climate, which enabled playing during colder months. The other was its demographic landscape and racial politics, which despite the presence of racism and segregation in amateur sports, offered openings for players excluded by the definitions of white manhood that governed U.S. leagues and venues. American athletes, both Black and white, traveled south, especially in winter and increasingly after Cuba gained independence in 1898, for opportunities to play and earn money. By the early twentieth century, the skill level in Cuba was competitive with that of the United States, and visiting Major Leaguers would play barnstorming games against their hosts, who more often than not prevailed.

The spread of baseball in the Americas over the twentieth century reflects Cuba's heavy imprint. Outside the United States and Canada, the places in the Western Hemisphere where baseball remains most popular—notably Panama, Puerto Rico, Venezuela, Colombia, the Dominican Republic, and Mexico—are Spanish-speaking countries or territories with coastlines on the Caribbean Sea that have had access to news from Cuba as the game flourished there. That common feature, rather than adjacency to the United States or the effects of U.S. foreign policy, is easily overlooked in accounts of the map of global baseball because most of those places also sit in the shadow of the United States. But an emphasis on U.S. sovereignty, hegemony, or proximity does not explain the history of baseball on the island of Hispaniola, for example. On the island's eastern side, baseball is the national pastime of the Dominican Republic; meanwhile, baseball has registered barely a ripple to the west, in Haiti. Language and historical connection to Cuba provide the keys to this mystery. Baseball did not develop a significant following in non-Spanish-speaking Caribbean lands that are geographically quite close to the United

States (the Bahamas, Jamaica), even countries with a history of prolonged U.S. military occupation (Haiti) or territories under U.S. sovereignty (the Virgin Islands). The only Caribbean island where baseball has thrived as a spectator sport without a historical connection to Spain is the small island of Curaçao—which now sends more players to the U.S. major leagues per capita than any country or territory in the world. But Curaçao is a telling exception. Both baseball and Spanish-language proficiency on the island reflect the influence and media presence of neighboring Venezuela during the twentieth century. On professional baseball fields, Curaçaoans generally speak Spanish.

In the current landscape of Caribbean baseball, Cuban influence is mostly a matter of history. After the overthrow of the Batista government in 1959, Cuba's place in the Latin American baseball world diminished, largely because the ensuing U.S. blockade kept players, equipment, and news from coming in and out of the island. The Havana Sugar Kings, a minor league affiliate of the Cincinnati Reds, lost their franchise to Jersey City. Revolutionary leader Fidel Castro, himself a baseball player (though popular legend exaggerates his pitching prowess with apocryphal claims that the Yankees offered him a tryout), sought in vain to keep the Sugar Kings in Cuba. Once that effort failed, Castro ended professional baseball, disbanding the Cuban League in 1961 and replacing it with the Serie Nacional de Béisbol. For the next several decades, Cuba would be the powerhouse of international amateur baseball competition. Meanwhile the epicenters of Latino baseball as a commercial spectator sport played by professionals and aspiring professionals moved to the U.S. Territory of Puerto Rico and, especially, the Dominican Republic.

Japan's baseball empire followed a more conventional course. Japanese educators and spectators embraced baseball quickly after 1871, when Hiraoka Hiroshi, co-father (along with American Horace Wilson) of Japanese baseball, traveled back to Japan from the United States and helped launch the game in a society that had no significant prior history of team sports. The earliest Japanese base-ball teams fielded amateurs, and competition between Tokyo's elite colleges, especially Waseda and Keio, attracted the greatest interest. The sport received a boost from high-profile visits from U.S. professional players beginning in 1907, culminating in the 1934 tour that included Babe Ruth, who was a major celebrity in Japan even prior to his arrival. But baseball remained an amateur affair, celebrated most conspicuously at the wildly popular Koshien high school tournament, beginning in 1915. Part of the explanation for the preeminence of amateur baseball in Japan lies in the fact that the sport was initially valued as a martial art and team-building discipline, rather than as a species of commercial entertainment, despite its thorough enmeshment in urban leisure and media culture.

Japanese public officials, like their U.S. counterparts, also saw the game as a civilizing instrument in the quest to build an overseas empire. When Japan colonized Taiwan (1895) and Korea (1910), baseball equipment and rulebooks arrived with colonial communities and figured in Japanese educational initiatives. Koreans had been introduced to the game slightly earlier by American missionaries, but Japan's colonial regime promoted baseball aggressively. In Taiwan, baseball was entirely associated with Japan, and in the early decades it was played mostly by Japanese colonists, for whom, in the words of one historian, "Taiwan became a satellite in the Japanese orbit within a wider baseball universe."[1] But by the 1920s, Taiwanese (both ethnic Chinese and aboriginal) were playing too, especially in schools, and the game became part of the colony's shared multiethnic culture. When Japanese colonization ended in both Korea and Taiwan following the Second World War, baseball remained popular, though efforts were made to efface or suppress reminders of its Japanese origins. In postwar Taiwan, the name of the sport was Sinicized (by tweaking a Chinese character) from *yakyū* to *banqiu*, but the baseball vocabulary, featuring English loan words such as *pitcha*, *kyatcha*, *homuran*, *sutoraiku*, and *hitto*, remained Japanese, despite a postcolonial

Figure 6.1 Americans of Japanese descent play baseball at the
Manzanar Relocation Center (California) where they were
incarcerated during the Second World War. Manzanar inmates
formed a dozen baseball leagues and fielded over one hundred teams,
including fourteen women's teams. Photographer Ansel Adams, who
produced this image, described Manzanar as "only a wartime detour
on the road to American citizenship," and he may have intended
photos like this to showcase Japanese eagerness to Americanize. But,
of course, the players (most of whom were in fact U.S. citizens) were
also playing the most popular team sport in Japan. *Library of
Congress, Prints & Photographs Division, Ansel Adams, photographer,
LC-DIG-ppprs-00369*

taboo against using Japanese words outside the ballfield. To this
day, East Asian baseball thrives especially in Japan's former colo-
nies and retains numerous marks of its development as a Japanese
imperial sport (Figure 6.1).

Meanwhile, in Japan under Allied occupation, professional
baseball took off. Nippon Professional Baseball (NPB; Nippon
Yakyū Kikō) was founded in 1949, with fifteen teams divided into

two leagues. It remains the dominant institution of organized team spectator sports in Japan and is among the most popular and broadly visible baseball organizations in the world. On the field of play, Japanese baseball has differed from North American and Caribbean baseball in subtle respects. Along with very minor rule variations and slight discrepancies in pitcher velocity, batter power, and outfield fence distance, managerial strategy favors more frequent recourse to bunts and other mechanisms for advancing baserunners by squandering outs or substituting players—though these differences have been exaggerated. Off the field, Japanese baseball teams have typically imposed more rigorous training and practice regimens. More striking differences are found in the stands, where the fan culture more nearly resembles that of American college football. Indeed, it was originally modeled on the football cheering practices that Tokyo's university teams had observed while visiting the United States in the early twentieth century. Musical bands, fight songs, and coordinated and ritualized revelry, periodically reinforced by female cheerleaders on the field, supply the ambiance at NPB games. Fans of the visiting team attend in significant numbers, seated with their own brass and percussion players in a separate cheering section.

Despite a distinctive ballpark culture, Japanese baseball fits squarely on the global baseball map and has exported the game to new frontiers, though now without the context of imperial conquest. Not long after guiding the Hanshin Tigers to their first Japan Series championship in 1985, team manager Yoshio Yoshida moved to France, where he spent six years promoting baseball and managing the French national team. More recently, Japanese institutions have cultivated ties with the growing baseball community in the Czech Republic. In 2023, the Panasonic Corporation announced its sponsorship of a cultural exchange and development program between the Chiba Lotte Marines of the Pacific League and Czech baseball. Japanese coaches and players have also been active in spreading the game to Brazil, where baseball was introduced in the early twentieth century by Japanese immigrants and where a training center is sponsored by the corporation that owns Tokyo's Yakult Swallows. In Brazil, baseball is more likely to be associated with Japan than with North America.

More famously, Japan has exported players to the United States. After Masanori Murakami debuted for the San Francisco Giants in 1964, no Japanese-born player cracked a Major League roster for another thirty years. But since the mid-1990s, numerous stars have made the jump, including Shohei Ohtani, who in 2024 signed a contract with the Los Angeles Dodgers that made him the highest-paid player in the history of professional baseball world-wide. Still, the bulk of the talent migration across the Pacific Ocean has gone, with less fanfare, in the other direction. For every Japanese who has played in top-level professional leagues in North America or the Caribbean, about ten U.S. or Caribbean players have entered the NPB, seeking opportunities for more playing opportunities or higher salaries. This disparity in the flow of play-ers is especially striking, given the fact that Japanese leagues restrict the number of foreigners who can appear on their rosters. The restriction reflects longstanding concerns that foreigners would dominate the sport, as well as perceptions, which have ebbed over the decades, that players from abroad don't understand the cul-ture of Japanese baseball and aren't sufficiently dedicated to its team ethos. In recent years, teams have often used at least part of their quota (currently four, though in the past it has generally been two or three) for large, Caribbean power hitters with some Major League Baseball experience.

One of those Caribbean power hitters, Wladimir Balentien of Curaçao, set Japan's single-season home run record in 2013, shat-tering a mark originally set almost fifty years earlier by the legend-ary Sadaharu Oh. Many in the Japanese baseball world had long bristled at the prospect of a foreigner displacing Oh, despite the irony that xenophobia had kept Oh (whose father was Taiwanese) himself from participating in the National Athletic Meet as a teenager. As manager of Tokyo's Giants, Oh sought to protect his record from foreign usurpation, reportedly fining his pitchers for every strike they threw to white American player Randy Bass of the Hanshin Tigers and intentionally walking him on the last day of the 1985 season when Bass was on the verge of tying Oh's total. But attitudes toward foreign players have softened over time, and Balentien's achievement was and is celebrated. Japanese-American outfielder Lars Nootbaar of the St. Louis Cardinals, who grew up in California and speaks little Japanese, became the first foreign-born player to represent Japan in international competition, and he now enjoys significant celebrity in his ancestral land.

Player movement in and out of Cuba, baseball's other historic center, has a more complicated history. After the abolition of professional baseball in 1961, foreigners had neither incentive nor opportunity to play in Cuba. Nor, for the most part, did the Castro regime allow Cubans to pursue opportunities on the international baseball market. Nonetheless, Cuba remained a conspicuous point of origin in the American baseball empire. Because so many players had signed in the major leagues prior to the revolution, it was still the case in the 1960s and 1970s that most of the Latino stars in U.S. baseball were Cuban. And in the 1980s, several standouts had been born in Havana, brought to the United States as infants, and raised in immigrant communities in Miami. Then, beginning in the 1990s, Cuban athletes began emigrating without authorization (and with considerable risk and sacrifice) to play in the United States, typically taking leave of their Cuban teams while engaged in international competitions. In fact, more Cuban defectors, as they are somewhat provocatively called, have appeared in major league uniform since the fall of the Soviet Union than all the Japanese-born players throughout history (Figure 6.2).

Despite this persistent clandestine migration, the world of Caribbean baseball that once orbited around Cuba is now largely identified with other islands, especially with the Dominican Republic, which is currently the birthplace of more MLB players and more foreign players in NPB than any country other than the

Figure 6.2 Cuban Premier Fidel Castro bats in front of a packed crowd in Havana to inaugurate the 1966 National Amateur Series. Baseball remains the island's national sport, but following the Castro-led revolution, it ceased to be played by professionals. *Alamy Images/Smith Archive*

United States. Select major league teams began scouting and developing young Dominican players in the 1970s, and their extraordinary success in signing future superstars at low cost prompted other franchises to follow suit. All thirty major league clubs now maintain baseball academies in the Dominican Republic, where promising teenagers are housed, fed, trained, and introduced to American culture. Though there was a time when the professional aspirations of a Spanish-speaking Caribbean baseball player might have focused on Cuba or Mexico, those who leave their homelands now (and many more remain) train their gaze on the United States and try to prepare for their careers by learning English.

As the most attractive magnet for talented players from several parts of the globe, professional baseball in the United States has highlighted issues surrounding immigration. A key moment in this history took place in 1981, when Fernando Valenzuela became baseball's dominant pitcher and led the Los Angeles Dodgers to a championship. Valenzuela, who had debuted the previous season at the age of nineteen, was the youngest of twelve children from a poor farming family of Mayo Indigenous descent in Sonora, Mexico. This part of Latin America had produced few baseball stars but many migrants to the Los Angeles area. While becoming a local hero and the anchor of the Dodgers' appeal to baseball's largest Chicano fan base, Valenzuela attracted widespread U.S. media attention to both his hometown and his personal journey as a teenaged immigrant who spoke no English. In subsequent decades, American baseball fans have immersed themselves in the study of visa restrictions, diasporic communities, acculturation challenges, and especially the language barriers that athletes encounter upon arrival. MLB teams employ full-time language interpreters, at least for Spanish, but the travails of Caribbean and East Asian players are standard fare in baseball reporting. Venezuelan infielder Wilmer Flores, who leaned on the TV series *Friends* to develop his English proficiency as a teenager in the U.S. minor leagues, honored that memory by selecting the show's theme song as his walk-up music when he reached the majors.

In this respect, the imperial role of the United States in global baseball remains singular and paramount. MLB exports the game to a vast and expanding set of foreign markets, mostly in the form of broadcasts and merchandise, but also by sending teams abroad to play. It also imports talent back to the game's metropolitan centers, seeks to integrate these players into its sporting culture, and then draws on their talent to elevate and enliven an entertainment product that can be reexported to future fans and players.

7

Color Lines

Frank Hart was the first Black U.S. athlete with an image on a piece of tradeable memorabilia. His appearance on an 1880 tobacco card reflected his celebrity as a world-champion speed walker who had just won a $21,000 prize for circling 565 miles around an indoor track in six days. Pedestrianism, as this sport was known, enjoyed brief but spectacular popularity in 1870s and 1880s America and Britain, and Hart was one of its shining stars. Less famously, Frank Hart also played baseball professionally, one of many Black Americans to do so in the nineteenth century, long before Jackie Robinson broke the color barrier in 1947 and officially ended baseball's Jim Crow era.

During the early decades of organized baseball, it remained uncertain how a sport that was anxiously protecting its claims to manhood would police its racial borders. White supremacy was built into many nineteenth-century Americans' conceptions of manhood; the claim of Black men to the title was in fact a pivotal issue in contemporary understandings of the Civil War. Black athletes had not been systematically excluded from athletic competition in the nineteenth century, before or after the war, but their success had been limited to individual sports such as boxing or (as in Frank Hart's case) racing. Baseball was distinctive among popular spectator sports in featuring teams, and the fraternal nature of its organization brought different racist pressures to bear. The original National Association of Base Ball Players resolved in 1867 to deny admission to any team "composed of one or more colored persons."[1] But the Association folded, and the professional leagues that followed made no such policy recommendations. Like many other sites and practices of segregation in the United States, the exclusion of Black baseball players took hold gradually and remained incomplete until the 1890s.

Several Black men excelled on overwhelmingly white professional teams in the 1870s and 1880s. Bud Fowler, who had the felicitous distinction of hailing from Cooperstown, was lauded in the sports press as "one of the best general players in the country."[2] Moses Fleetwood Walker played one season in the American Association (a major league) and later in the International League, where multiple Black players tested the limits of white racism against a backdrop of shifting U.S. race relations at the end of the Reconstruction Era.

But as legal segregation took hold in the South, baseball's color line hardened in the northern cities where professional baseball flourished. International League teams began releasing and barring Black players in 1887, and within a few years professional baseball was fully segregated. In popular histories of the sport's transition, much is made of the racism of Cap Anson, player-manager of the Chicago White Stockings. Anson, a white Iowan who grew up among the Potawatomi Indian nation, threatened to withdraw from an exhibition game in Newark if the home team's Black pitcher took the mound. The impact of Anson's defiant stand is easily exaggerated, but the story accurately captures the fact that players, rather than management or consumers, led the charge to rid professional baseball of Black presence. Team executives generally sought talent wherever they could find it, especially if it could be acquired less expensively. White fans, for their part, did not threaten to boycott teams that employed Blacks, and in fact they often cheered them on. But white players, invoking codes of manly honor, would petition their employers to keep their rosters white. Until they succeeded, they frequently ostracized Black teammates, typically excluding them from team photos. On the field, Black players endured opponents' attempts to injure them with spikes, while teammates sabotaged their play and altered game records to diminish their statistical achievements. A white pitcher recalled ignoring the signals of Walker, who had been "the best catcher I ever worked with," because he "disliked a Negro."[3] By 1892, the exclusion of Black men from professional baseball leagues, often referred to as a Gentleman's Agreement, was an accomplished fact.

Baseball's color line remained in place for more than half a century. No Black player was signed to any team in either the major or minor leagues during that period, though several clubs hired Black men as mascots, typically in demeaning roles that undermine the arguments of those who see racial mascot figures as historically benign. Cincinnati's team employed a man named Clarence Duval and brought him along on their 1889 international tour. Players would rub Duval's head in the dugout for good luck. On the playing field, however, Black presence was unwelcome.[4]

Still, baseball's color line was subject to perpetual pressures, the result of ambiguities in racial identity and classification and the occasional desire of management to sneak talented nonwhite players under the radar of white racial anxieties. The primary threats to the color line came from baseball's spread to parts of the country and hemisphere where racial taxonomies and hierarchies differed as a consequence of varying histories of European colonization, African slavery, and postcolonial nationbuilding.

The case of Vincent Irwin Nava, the first Mexican American to play in the majors, illustrates the way U.S. leagues navigated these conditions. Nava was born Vincente Simental to a Mexican mother in San Francisco in 1850, two years after the United States claimed sovereignty over what had been part of the Republic of Mexico. Under the terms of the treaty that ended the U.S.-Mexican War, Mexicans of Indigenous, African, or mixed descent were entitled to naturalize as U.S. citizens, despite the fact that federal law restricted naturalization to "free white persons," making Mexicans an anomalous and liminal racial category in U.S. law and politics. The Simental family moved south to what was still

Mexico, and then came back to San Francisco, where Vincente's mother married Englishman William Irwin and raised the boy in California as Vincent Irwin. But when Irwin was recruited from a minor league in California to play catcher for the Providence Grays, he presented himself as Vincent Sandy Nava. The impulse to Hispanicize his surname seems to have come from Providence's management, which hoped to generate interest in a player with exotic Spanish origins, but it also served to preempt unwelcome speculation about his racial identity. Team owners saw ethnic difference as a selling point, so long as players remained within the racial boundaries typically policed by white teammates.[5] Management was also open to Native American players, while both demanding that they be light-skinned and acculturated to white American society and exploiting their racial difference for profit. Indigenous players like Charles Albert "Chief" Bender were given tokenizing nicknames that emphasized ethnic difference while reducing them to stereotypes.

Establishing and maintaining racial segregation was made more difficult by Latin America's complex racial landscape, specifically in Cuba, the capital of Caribbean baseball. When baseball first arrived in Cuba in 1864, the Spanish colony was still importing captives from Africa, and slavery remained legal on the island for another twenty years (long after it had been abolished in much of the Americas). Unlike the situation in many Latin American lands, where a majority of the population had some Indigenous ancestry, Cuban society was racially stratified across a spectrum of skin color that signified degrees of African descent. Census records distinguished a white (*blanco*) population of Iberian immigrants and their creolized descendants from a nonwhite (*colorado*) population composed of Africans and those descended primarily or partially from Africans. Racial segregation existed in Cuban society to a much greater extent than in Central America or Mexico, but the category of white was not as narrowly defined in Cuba as it was in the United States. In the United States at the end of the nineteenth

Figure 7.1 In 1901, a Black second baseman named Charlie Grant signed with the Baltimore Orioles, which at the time was a member of the upstart American League, before the franchise moved to New York and eventually became the Yankees. Manager John McGraw hoped to be able to put a Black player on the field by claiming he was a Cherokee named Chief Tokahoma. In addition to taking advantage of the fact that Indigenous Americans were allowed in the majors, McGraw, who lived part-time in the Southeast, understood that many people of African descent claimed membership in nations such as the Seminole, Creek, and Cherokee. But when rival owners learned that McGraw and Grant were trying to skirt the unwritten ban on Black players, they cried foul, forcing Baltimore to abandon the plan and denying Grant the chance to become the first Black player in the American League. *SABR-Rucker Archive*

century, *any* African descent marked a person as Black and subject to discrimination and exclusion.

Although the first Cuban professional played in the United States in 1868, the significant arrival of Cubans to the major leagues began forty years later. From the start, players from Cuba were scrutinized for signs of possible Blackness. Club management sought to burnish evidence—or simply insisted—that the players they were signing were "pure Spaniards, without a trace of colored blood," or "having more Spanish blood in him than Cuban," or, even more specifically, "the *purest bars of Castilian soap* that ever floated to these shores." In identifying a Cuban baseball player with the Iberian Peninsula, the place where Western ideas of blood purity originated, white managers, scouts, and journalists were both limiting the range of Latino players who might be allowed on U.S. teams and clarifying baseball's color lines. But the sometimes hostile and suspicious attitudes of white fans and teammates to the players suggested that those lines remained blurry.

Viewed from the U.S. mainland, Cuba could represent a tool or foil for attacking segregation. A Black barnstorming team calling itself the Cuban Giants (featuring zero players from Cuba) formed in 1885 and became the leading Black professional club before the advent of the Negro Leagues. The name "Cuban" might have been an attempt to downplay or even conceal the players' racial identity in Jim Crow America, but the club was also deploying Cuba as a figure for mixed-race status and a reminder that in nearby Cuba people of African descent played professional baseball alongside whites. To Black American baseball players, Cuban baseball held promise and opportunity. Although amateur leagues in Cuba maintained some degree of racial segregation, professional baseball was integrated. Beginning in 1900, Black players, both U.S. and Caribbean, began wintering in the Cuban League. Over the course of the 1920s and 1930s, the biggest names in Negro League baseball all appeared in Cuban League uniform. Black U.S. stars also played in Puerto Rico, Mexico, and the Dominican Republic.

Whereas Caribbean baseball welcomed Black Americans, dark-skinned players from the Caribbean were barred from white leagues in the United States. Instead, many of them pursued opportunities in organized Black baseball. Independent Black professional clubs had played against white opponents and one another, though always as stand-alone entertainment. In 1920, Rube Foster, a former star pitcher and the innovative manager of one of those clubs, created the Negro National League, the first of several Negro Leagues that thrived over the next three decades. Foster preached racial solidarity and self-reliance but did not envision his league as a separatist project. Instead, he hoped to steer Black fan patronage to Black-owned businesses while ultimately paving the way for integration by demonstrating the quality of the Black game. Foster achieved this in part by introducing a more exciting style of play that featured stolen bases, drag bunts, and other displays of speed and athleticism, but mostly by attracting the crowds and attention that league structure, championships, and partisan fan loyalties could generate.

Negro League games featuring outstanding Black American and Latino players proved immediately popular in northern and midwestern cities where the Great Migration had swelled Black populations during and after the First World War. But at no point did Negro League teams make enough money to confine their play to league competition. Instead, they relied on revenue from exhibition tours and additional games against myriad opponents throughout the country. White fans were scarce at official Negro League games, and Black attendance on any day other than Sunday tended to be modest as well. Still, Negro League baseball quickly became a central institution of Black urban life. The spectacular successes of the 1924 Colored World Series between the champions of the Negro National League and the Eastern Colored League, and then the East-West All-Star Game in the 1930s, demonstrated the sport's immense appeal. Meanwhile, the victories of Negro

League stars in barnstorming competition against major league teams demonstrated parity between Black and white baseball.

Support for integrating organized baseball increased significantly over the course of the Second World War, as Black and white Americans linked wartime aims and postwar national interests with the cause of racial equality. The prospects of integration also benefited from the death in 1944 of Kenesaw Mountain Landis, organized baseball's first commissioner, whose longstanding resistance to integration had posed a formidable obstacle. With Landis out of the way, Branch Rickey, general manager of the Brooklyn Dodgers, pursued the experiment of signing Jackie Robinson of the Kansas City Monarchs to a contract in 1947. In the face of vociferous and sometimes violent hostility from a minority of fans and opponents, Robinson was a big success on the field. Rickey signed additional young Negro League stars, and other teams began doing the same. By the mid-1960s most of the superstars in Major League Baseball were men who would have been (or had been) barred twenty years earlier. Meanwhile, the Negro Leagues, whose teams were not compensated for the loss of players under contract, suffered. By 1960, the last remaining league folded.

In recent decades, Major League Baseball has vigorously promoted the legacy of both the sport's integration and the Negro Leagues that integration helped destroy. As of 1997, all thirty MLB teams retired Jackie Robinson's uniform number, which means that it will never be assigned to anyone else—an honor that no other professional sport has bestowed on any player. Every April 15, however, which is the anniversary of Robinson's MLB debut (and officially Jackie Robinson Day in the league since 2005), every single player, coach, and umpire on the field dons the now iconic number 42. In the 1970s, the Hall of Fame in Cooperstown began inducting former Negro League stars, and in 2020 baseball authorities acknowledged those associations as major leagues.

Finally, in 2024, MLB decreed that the achievements of Negro League players belonged in the majors' official record books.

This project of restorative justice has unfolded against the backdrop of a crisis in the game's relationship to Black America. The proportion of MLB players who are Black dropped steadily toward the end of the twentieth century and is significantly below that of basketball and football. More worrisome to league officials, but certainly not unrelated, was the fact that Black fans seemed less interested than ever in the sport. The trend toward lower Black attendance already became apparent in some cities in the 1980s with the rising popularity of the NBA, and it accelerated after the turn of the century as baseball ticket prices rose. By 2014, stadium crowds were less than 5 percent Black. Around that time, outfielder Curtis Granderson described a game he would play with Black teammates as they scanned the stands at Yankee Stadium and other venues for African American spectators. "'I see one! No, he's Latino.' You're panning, panning, and sometimes it would take us seven innings to count 10."[6] The decline in Black engagement extends beyond the ballpark. A 2023 survey found that half of Black respondents in the United States identified as "not a fan" of baseball, compared to only 15 percent calling themselves "avid fans."[7] A sport that had been at the center of Black cultural life for much of the twentieth century—and played a conspicuous symbolic role in race relations and civil rights politics—suddenly seemed more marginal.

None of this amounts to a reimposition of baseball's color line, of course, or even the whitening of baseball. Part of the change has to do with the prominence of Latinx players and fans. As Granderson's account indicates, a Latino spectator might have initially been identified as Black but then had to be excluded from the count to make the point. Roberto Clemente, the star Puerto Rican outfielder for the Pittsburgh Pirates who was killed in a 1972 plane crash and who is the only player other than Robinson canonized by the league as a figure of racial inclusion and social consciousness, stands more for his Latino than for his Black identity. Many dark-skinned players like Clemente, both North American and Caribbean, who would have been barred from the field before integration now get classified as Brown—and African American fans do not identify with them. But Latinx fans do, and they are numerous. The same 2023 poll that showed higher rates of baseball interest among white Americans than Black Americans revealed even higher engagement among those who identified as Hispanic: two out of three called themselves fans of the game, and 36 percent described that fandom as "avid."

The legacy of white racism undoubtedly persists in organized U.S. baseball, as does the legacy of xenophobia in Japanese baseball, and in both cases the persistence is built into codes of manly honor that enjoin restraint and disparage certain kinds of display. But whereas manhood codes have managed to exclude women, they have not succeeded in maintaining baseball as the preserve of a single ethnicity or culture. Although baseball originated among players and spectators who were English-speaking, white, mostly Protestant Americans, it quickly spread beyond those bounds. Twenty-first-century global baseball is composed predominantly of people—performers and spectators—who belong to none of those demographic categories.

8

Labor and Capital

In June 1972, just two years after his appointment by President Richard Nixon to the U.S. Supreme Court, Associate Justice Harry A. Blackmun produced a lengthy majority opinion in a case entitled *Flood v. Kuhn*. Blackmun is better remembered for what he wrote six months later, when he crafted the Court's *Roe v. Wade* decision, which for the next half-century would protect the rights of women to terminate pregnancies. His 1972 ruling, by contrast, had little influence on subsequent jurisprudence and is hardly a judicial landmark. But it stands as one of the most elaborate and pious statements of the federal government on the subject of baseball. Asked to weigh in on MLB's longstanding exemption from antitrust laws and the legality of its restrictive player contract provisions, Blackmun opened his ruling with his take on the sport.

After surveying highlights of baseball history and lore, the opinion listed famous players, eighty-eight of them in all (a first draft had included twelve fewer), whom Blackmun deemed worthy of mention and cited popular poems about the sport. It was an oddly self-indulgent preamble by the Court's biggest baseball fan, which concurring Justice Byron White (a former professional football player) considered beneath the dignity of the judiciary. Nor did it relate directly to what followed. Blackmun, on behalf of a five to three majority, ruled that although the logic of earlier decisions upholding baseball's immunity from antitrust action was flawed, those decisions had been settled law for long enough that only Congress, through special legislation, could withdraw the exemption.

Though the constitutional issues in the case involved antitrust policy and interstate commerce, the underlying conflict that ultimately put the Supreme Court in the unusual position of celebrating baseball was fundamentally about labor relations. The precipitating cause was the refusal of outfielder Curt Flood to accept a trade in 1969 from the St. Louis Cardinals to the Philadelphia Phillies. Flood, a Black man from Oakland, California, claimed that the power of Major League Baseball to determine his place of employment without his consent reduced his status to that of a "well-paid slave"—a particularly powerful charge in the wake of a civil rights revolution in U.S. law and politics and in the context of a rising Black Power movement—and he chose to sue the league. The broader context was the emergence of a powerful players union in the 1960s under the spectacularly effective leadership of former United Steelworkers negotiator Marvin Miller. The revitalized union supported Flood's suit, while simultaneously driving owners to the negotiating table with credible strike threats. Baseball's first collective bargaining agreement was signed in 1970, between Flood's refusal to report to Philadelphia and Blackmun's decision in the court case (Figure 8.1).

Ultimately, the cause of the conflict lay in a longstanding and interesting feature of modern professional team sports, not unique to baseball, which structures relations between labor and capital. Talented individual athletes are distinctively positioned to entertain spectators, but in a game like baseball they cannot perform alone. They are dependent not only on teammates, but also on some sort of management to provide the theatrical venues and competitive infrastructure needed to display their talent. Because paying spectators want to watch closely fought contests and also to see their favored teams prevail, teams are incentivized both to recruit the best players and to allow their opponents to do so (to a certain extent) as well. While encouraging collusion to avoid an expensive arms race, this situation also creates some ambiguity as to whether the real employer—and the real entertainment

Figure 8.1 Curt Flood paints the late Martin Luther King Jr. Having sacrificed his career to challenge baseball's labor regime beginning in 1969, Flood saw his own crusade as part of a larger struggle for equality and justice. Significantly, the two retired major league stars who stood up for Flood, Hank Greenberg (Jewish) and Jackie Robinson (Black), had both been subjected to bigotry and racial animus during their careers, and they accordingly viewed Flood's challenge as a civil rights issue. *AP Photo/Fred Waters*

product—is the team or the league. Such considerations, along with the more ubiquitous desire of business owners to maximize profits by reducing wages, help explain why baseball clubs saw fit to introduce the infamous "reserve clause" in their player contracts in the 1870s, and why Congress and the courts saw fit for almost a century to shield these contracts from legal scrutiny.

In its initial form, the reserve clause was an attempt by the new National League to establish continuity and cultivate partisan fan allegiances by limiting player movement between teams. Clubs could designate (reserve) five of their contracted players, who would be off-limits to negotiations with other teams. Just four years after its introduction, the reserve rule was expanded to include most or all of a team's roster, allowing employers to extend a player's contractual obligations unilaterally for a full year after the contract expired, which effectively prevented players from signing elsewhere in the league unless they were willing to sit out (without pay) an entire season and risk being blacklisted upon their return. These club-friendly contracts were also transferable, which meant that a player could be bought, sold, and exchanged at the will of his employer. While radically limiting the freedom of players to choose where to play and live, the reservation system also put uniquely talented performers in a weak bargaining position. Instead of simply negotiating with a team that had to balance the goals of cutting costs and winning championships, players were negotiating with a league of colluding employers whose shared interest in cutting costs converged with their shared interest in maintaining competitive balance.

The real threat to this system, from the perspective of the business owners, lay in the prospect of other leagues whose franchises would not be bound to honor National League contracts and could therefore sign players who chose to hold out. For this reason, the same year that NL owners expanded the reserve clause, they also negotiated an agreement with the other two major leagues (the American Association and the Northwestern League) to honor one another's contracts. The rise of John Montgomery Ward's short-lived Players' League in 1891 offered a beacon of hope to baseball's laboring class, not only because players could reap a share of club profits, but mostly because the existence of a major league unbound by the reserve clauses of its competitors knocked the teeth out of those clauses, giving players negotiating leverage and a measure of free agency. But with the Players' League out of the way, a new agreement in place between the National and American Leagues, and no serious rivalry to their joint dominance of the market for baseball entertainment, major league owners controlled their labor costs during the first half of the twentieth century with little resistance or interference.

For U.S. professionals, the only paths out of the reserve system led abroad, but the international game offered few options. East Asian baseball remained a primarily amateur affair, and most Caribbean leagues played in the winter, providing opportunities for Black American players excluded from the Majors and enabling white Americans to earn some extra money during their offseason but little in the way of negotiating leverage with their employers. (Dominican teams occasionally lured Negro Leaguers south, notably during the Trujillo regime in the late 1930s, but in any case Negro Leagues never imposed reserve clauses.) The one foreign league that threatened to unsettle MLB labor relations was in Mexico. The wealthy Pasquel family, which owned all eight Mexican League teams, raided U.S. rosters in 1946, luring star players from the Giants, Cardinals, and Dodgers south with salary offers more than double what they were getting paid. Major League Commissioner Happy Chandler declared war on the Mexican League and imposed five-year bans on any player who signed with their teams. As that league struggled, some of the players sought to return and initiated lawsuits. Eager to avoid further trouble, Chandler offered amnesty to all defectors, and by 1950 the major leagues' labor system had survived its most serious foreign challenge. Not until the 1980s would salary offers from other countries figure in MLB labor relations, and in that instance Japan's own restrictions on foreign players minimized the impact.

While the reserve clause allowed clubs to suppress salaries for established players without fear of competition, management also needed to control labor costs for entry-level players. The most successful strategy for doing so involved the creation of farm systems in the minor leagues. Developed in the 1920s and 1930s by Branch Rickey during his tenure as general manager of the Cardinals, this system entailed major league corporations buying or investing in affiliated minor league franchises and assigning them players under contract to the parent club. The arrangement boosted interest in the minor leagues, but more significantly it allowed teams in the Majors to train, develop, and audition young players without having to pay them major league salaries and without having to bid for their services when they ultimately proved ready for top-level play. Other owners followed Rickey's lead, and by 1940 organized baseball was a vertically integrated operation with a uniform employment structure through which owners could limit how much money went to performers.

Counterbalancing the owners' collective interest in controlling costs was their competition to win games and championships. Though owners could stand united in opposition to labor, the nature of their enterprise put them at odds with one another on the playing field and in the standings. And since they did not pool revenue, beating other teams was not simply a point of pride; it translated into a greater share of the profits of baseball entertainment. Such competition exerted upward pressures on player salaries because general managers might calculate that a small extra investment in payroll would produce a championship and thereby yield a much bigger slice of the revenue that baseball generated.

Clubs were also tempted to look beyond the traditional sources of talent in search of cheaper alternatives. This is an underappreciated factor in the history of baseball's racial integration. It is not coincidental that the same Branch Rickey, whose innovative development of minor league affiliates helped build dominant teams in St. Louis before the Second World War, was also the executive whose pioneering signing of Black players helped build dominant teams in Brooklyn after the war. What linked the two moves was Rickey's willingness to do something novel that would enable a team to sign outstanding players without breaking the corporate bank. In integrating the National League, Rickey raided Negro League teams that he did not have to compensate. In subsequent decades, clubs would seek similar advantages by scouting and signing young players in other countries. The Washington

Senators pioneered this strategy successfully in Cuba in the 1950s, and later the Los Angeles Dodgers and Toronto Blue Jays found similar success in the Dominican Republic. As with Rickey's signing of Jackie Robinson, these moves precipitated trends that eventually diminished the competitive advantages that the innovators had achieved—and also negated some the cost savings that they had exploited.

In responding to the initiatives of the most successful clubs, other owners invoked the ideal of competitive balance, which they knew was part of the economic value of baseball as entertainment. Dodgers, Cardinals, and Yankees might have reaped benefits from winning so many pennants in the middle third of the century, but they had a financial stake in other teams putting competitive teams on the field. In 1965, Major League Baseball introduced an amateur draft, something that had been used already by other sports leagues, to distribute players from high school, college, and other nonprofessional teams more evenly across the sport. Drafts and other efforts to impose or restore balance among teams in a sports league (including salary caps and revenue pooling) generally help poorer clubs and their fan bases, but they undermine the financial interests of players by limiting the free market for players' services. The prospect of competitive *imbalance*, in other words, is what tempts a club to raise player pay. The goal of balance justifies rules that remove that temptation or prohibit acting upon it.

At the end of the 1960s, then, when Curt Flood sued Major League Baseball, the balance of power between labor and capital in U.S. professional baseball was tilted dramatically in favor of club owners. The reserve clause prevented players from pursuing better offers, no foreign leagues presented options, integration in the major leagues and the death of Cuban professional baseball brought more competition for roster spots and created a buyers' market for baseball labor, and the amateur draft bound players to clubs not of their choosing before they started their careers. The players had one major advantage, of course: notably, they, and not their employers, could play the game at a level that would attract mass spectatorship. But that longstanding advantage had not been decisive in the past, and in 1970 there was no obvious reason to suspect that it ever would.

The tilting of the negotiating tables in the other direction over the course of a decade is largely a story of an unusually successful union. Marvin Miller managed to persuade players with different salaries and circumstances that they shared a common interest, and those players presented a unprecedentedly unified front. Flood's legal challenge died in 1972 in Washington, but the support he received from fellow Major Leaguers and in the court of public opinion put pressure on the league. The Court seemed to be inviting Congress to reconsider baseball's antitrust exemption, and Blackmun's ruling proved a pyrrhic victory for the owners. Commissioner Bowie Kuhn's rhetorical stance that the conflict over the reserve clause could be resolved in labor negotiations (rather than imposed by the courts) forced owners to the bargaining table, where they faced a formidable adversary. Miller got the owners to submit contract disputes to binding arbitration, arbitration panels sided with the union on more limited constructions of reserve clauses, and a few high-profile players were declared free agents and received much higher salaries. Using short work stoppages in the early 1970s to force improvements to the basic agreement between the union and the league, Miller negotiated a seeming compromise on the reserve clause that wound up benefiting players. Players would be bound to teams for an initial six-year period, which had the effect of limiting the supply of free agents in any given season, thereby driving up the salary offers they would receive, and in turn setting higher benchmarks and pay scales that would be cited in the salary arbitration hearings of other players.

These union victories ushered in an era of free agency in organized U.S. baseball but not an era of labor peace. Frequent strikes and lockouts, including stoppages that canceled substantial parts of the 1981 and 1994 seasons, mostly hinged on attempts by owners to restore control over salaries by imposing compensation for teams that lose players to free agency or by setting limits to salaries. These efforts mostly failed. Players proved unified in their willingness to strike, and owners ultimately proved unwilling to risk devaluing their franchises by allowing seasons to be canceled and fans to be permanently alienated. And though clubs have frequently complained that they lose money, they have never been willing to open their books to demonstrate this loss. The skyrocketing valuations of their businesses also dwarf any operations losses that they could conceivably sustain. Moreover, all it takes is one team owner paying top dollar to a free agent to undermine any shared interest in depressing salaries.

In the 1990s, the players also won legal victories that further undermined the owners' position. In 1995, federal judge Sonia Sotomayor (who would eventually supplant Harry Blackmun as the most vocal baseball fan in the history of the Supreme Court) filed an injunction against the owners' bid to end free agency and imposed a salary cap, thereby ending the devastating strike that had wiped out the 1994 World Series. Four years later, Congress passed the Curt Flood Act, officially ending the exemption from antitrust laws that baseball (alone among U.S. professional team sports) had enjoyed and that Flood's suit had sought to nullify.

The Major League Baseball Players Association continues to be a powerful actor in the economic landscape of organized sports. It does not negotiate player contracts (that job belongs to private agents who form another important class in baseball's labor relations), but it does regulate working conditions through collective bargaining agreements and weighs in on every detail of MLB rules. The union has secured countless benefits for its membership, including a minimum salary of close to $800,000 per year, and the effect of free agency has been to generate a top annual salary (for Shohei Ohtani) about seventy times what the highest-paid player (Willie Mays) received in 1970, adjusted for inflation. Baseball's union has successfully prevented the imposition of the salary caps that are in place in professional football, soccer, hockey, and basketball in the United States. Those other team sports have player unions as well, as does Japanese baseball, but none boasts the same record of success.

Union strength may be especially important to baseball players because even the best ones have fewer opportunities to make millions in endorsement deals than their counterparts in the NBA or in international soccer, let alone those in individual sports. Certain structural features of baseball deemphasize the power of the single athlete: most scoring and most scoring prevention require contributions from more than one player (the contrast with basketball is clearest), and the one player in a position to exert the greatest impact on a game's outcome, the starting pitcher, appears only every fifth game (every sixth in Japanese baseball) and is especially susceptible to long-term injury. The addition of a single superstar is rarely sufficient to elevate a mediocre team's fortunes. All of this shapes baseball's economics as well as its strategic character and its appeal to fans and bettors.

The prominence of union regulations and negotiations in organized baseball has familiarized fans with lockouts, labor relations boards, and judicial injunctions. But most observers find it difficult to see baseball's labor disputes as class conflict. Both sides now appear to possess significant wealth (though that is less true of the minor leaguers who are now also represented by the union or the marginal Major Leaguers with short careers). Moreover, the union's position is resolutely capitalist and free-market (players should be free agents and deserve whatever some owner is willing to pay them), whereas the owners speak of balance, equity, limits, and sharing. Nonetheless, professional ballplayers are employees under contractual obligation, and their wealth is the product of collective bargaining rather than simply the proceeds of commercial entertainment.

Like the most popular entertainers in other fields, such as Taylor Swift, George Clooney, Oprah Winfrey, or Rafael Nadal, highly paid baseball players in the United States, Japan, Venezuela, and the Dominican Republic are celebrities with agents who secure for them the best possible share of the profits they generate. But unlike those other celebrities (even those who technically belong to unions), a long and high-profile history of conflict between employers and employees in the United States has played a dominant role in shaping their compensation. Fans who don't think twice about the earnings of Winfrey or Clooney often gasp at Shohei Ohtani's $70 million annual salary, in large part because Ohtani is a salaried employee, whereas other kinds of entertainers are seen as entrepreneurs. And Ohtani is an employee for a reason. His form of entertainment, modern team sports, dictates in some sense that he be seen as such.

At the other extreme from American organized baseball, which has made millionaires of hundreds of U.S., Japanese, and Dominican athletes, stands Cuba, where star athletes are given *licencia deportiva* to take off time from work to hone their skills but are not otherwise compensated. Castro's Cuba, as a semi-official magazine of the regime put it in 1961, "eradicated the practice of professional baseball, considering it a form of the exploitation of man by man."[1] Perhaps Curt Flood and Marvin Miller might have sympathized with part of the premise, but the model of free agency they championed saw the release from exploitation within the entertainment marketplace rather than in opposition to it.

9

Spectacle and Media

Like most sports and many other forms of modern entertainment, baseball has always depended on live audiences, not just for revenue, but as a fundamental part of its character. Without an engaged crowd, a baseball game is just a recreational activity. Yet on-site spectators represent only a small fraction of a baseball audience. The competition in the ballpark attracts intense interest in part because numerous people elsewhere follow its progress and attune to its outcome. Most of that attunement is mediated or deferred. The paid attendance at a given game reflects fan interest cultivated over time and across space as fans watch games from afar, read about teams in news reports, and discuss players at work, in classrooms, over drinks, and at dinner tables. Still, the fans in the stands are a crucial part of the spectacle itself. When the COVID pandemic kept fans out of the ballpark in 2020, Major League Baseball simulated their presence by placing cardboard cutouts in empty seats.

From its earliest years, the spectacle of baseball depended on media. Printed news reports in the middle of the nineteenth century did more than just alert fans to the timing and location of games; they gave meaning to those games. Sports papers in New York in the 1850s or in Havana in the 1870s assigned significance to outcomes and credit (or blame) to players and teams. In the process, they created an audience that vastly exceeded the number of spectators on hand for a particular performance, much as those same newspapers often did for the theater. Fans followed baseball in the press, where they encountered capsule narratives in the form of the celebrated box score, introduced already in the 1850s.

Newspapers, aided by the telegraph network, also enabled fans to follow games in real time. As professional baseball grew in popularity around the beginning of the twentieth century, news offices would display live updates to assembled crowds. These displays, anticipating some of the modes through which fans now follow games in progress on their smartphones, might feature bells and colored lights to indicate balls, strikes, and outs, and represented the movements of ball and players with magnetic pieces. The history of baseball broadcasting, in other words, is quite long, and it began with newspapers and telegraphs, rather than radio and television.

Still, the rapid spread of radio broadcasting and transistor radio ownership in the United States during the early 1920s heralded a new era in the history of entertainment, and Major League Baseball was the first sport to demonstrate radio's immense power. A live, play-by-play, eyewitness description of the 1922 World Series between New York's Giants and Yankees, delivered over WJZ radio by the legendary sportswriter Grantland Rice to an estimated five million listeners, was celebrated in the press as "the greatest audience ever assembled to listen to one man."[1]

Many in the baseball world feared what radio broadcasts portended for the sport, which was enjoying a peak of popularity with the emergence of superstar home run hitter Babe Ruth. Concerned that stadium attendance might suffer, New York City banned radio broadcasts of baseball games from 1924 to 1929, and St. Louis did the same in 1934. The *Sporting News*, noting in 1922 that "this new radio craze is already crimping attendance…[at] spectacular entertainment," envisioned a day when fans would have no reason to go to the ballpark at all. "When Ruth hits a homer or [George] Sisler slides into the plate," the article predicted, "a film will catch him in the act, wireless will carry it a thousand miles broadcast and the family sitting in the darkened living room at home will see the scene reproduced instantaneously on the wall." In that event, the glorious urban stadiums "will be torn down and the business of baseball will be collecting a fee for supplying the action that is reproduced on the parlor wall instead of counting the gate."[2]

Predictions that broadcasting would reshape spectator sports were certainly fulfilled in the ensuing decades, but the prophecies of doom were not. For one thing, as the *Sporting News* acknowledged, fans would still want to watch games remotely and pay for the privilege. For another, broadcasting, much like earlier newspaper summaries, telegraph relays, and visual reenactments, tended to stoke rather than sate interest in live spectatorship. During the second quarter of the twentieth century, radio broadcasts expanded the reach of live games far beyond city limits. Stations in Chicago and St. Louis emitted powerful signals across vast swathes of Wisconsin, Iowa, Nebraska, and South Dakota, pushing Major League Baseball's western frontier and building loyalties that would endure for generations. Broadcasts from Cuba created fan bases for teams from Havana and Almendares across the Caribbean basin.[3] As for those living closer to urban ballparks, the awareness of massive remote audiences enhanced the appeal of live attendance, much as would happen later in the century with televised entertainment.

The compatibility and synergy of live baseball and mass broadcasting, clear enough in retrospect, emerged only gradually. The story might be told as a process by which the major leagues adjusted to various technological innovations that spread during the second quarter of the twentieth century, including radio, television, and air travel. But this adjustment was a contested embrace of a new entertainment landscape. A key figure in the embrace was the entrepreneurial executive Larry MacPhail. Though he is also remembered for his later resistance to baseball's racial integration, MacPhail earned a place in the Hall of Fame for championing such innovations as night games, player pension plans, batting helmets, and luxury stadium seating, while reviving the sagging fortunes of franchises in Cincinnati, Brooklyn, and the Bronx. MacPhail's varied claims to fame might obscure a prevailing preoccupation: he saw baseball first and foremost as a species of spectacular entertainment.

Controversies over night games brought MacPhail's approach to baseball as spectacle into full view. Against the avowed opposition of a powerful commissioner and the resistance of several club owners, he secured permission to have lights installed in the Cincinnati Reds' ballpark in 1935 and staged a ceremony in which President Roosevelt illuminated Crosley Field remotely by telegraph signal. Electric lighting was hardly a novel technology in the 1930s, but it was part of MacPhail's larger strategic response to the rise of broadcasting, which he also supported enthusiastically. MacPhail sought to expand the daily reach of his entertainment product beyond the ballpark while highlighting what was uniquely compelling about attending a live game. Whereas an owner in the American League (which waited several years before following MacPhail's lead) charged that night baseball would spell the sport's "ruination" by transforming "players from athletes to actors," MacPhail understood that athletes were already actors. This connection had been highlighted for American moviegoers since the 1920s by the frequent appearance of baseball games in theatrical film reels and coverage of the cinematic career of Babe Ruth, which began while he was still playing for the Yankees. "Sooner or later, the game will be played in its entirety at night," MacPhail proclaimed, and "then baseball will be squarely in the amusement, the entertainment business along with wrestling, midget car racing and the trotting tracks."[4] Baseball's even closer neighbors in the entertainment business were drama, comedy, dance, music, and news, which were consumed during this era in many of the same venues and through the same media.

The first (relatively primitive) televised game broadcasts took place in New York in 1939 during that city's World's Fair, not long into the era of baseball on the radio. But television did not begin to rival radio as a medium for consuming baseball until after the Second World War. By the 1950s, national networks were showing the same game in real time to audiences across the country and were shaping the business of both baseball and broadcasting. As had radio, television reached fans who had never attended a ballpark and reoriented the geography of baseball attention and fan loyalty. More generally and obviously, the expanded reach of networks, cable channels, and eventually internet streaming, with their tight command of viewer attention, would turn media rights into the largest source of revenue for baseball franchises and televised broadcasts and replays into the dominant format in which fans experience game action (Figure 9.1).

Radio and television offer different experiences of live baseball action. Radio broadcasts began as simple eyewitness narration and to a large extent that's what they remain: two people sit at the ballpark and describe the action to fans who are not there. For rapt listeners, however, it is typically the sounds as much as the verbal content that make the broadcast. Those sounds include the enthusiastic tones of the avowedly partisan model spectators hired to offer commentary from the booth. But the two most compelling and indicative sounds that are immediately and faithfully transmitted are the spontaneous roar of the home crowd (as with radio broadcasts of most live sporting events) and the singular sound of bat on ball. That sound has no counterpart in soccer, basketball, hockey, or U.S. football.

The overwhelming advantage of a television broadcast, of course, is that baseball is a spectacle. And like many sports, baseball features numerous visibly close plays and visual judgments (balls and strikes, fair and foul balls, tag plays at home plate) in which spectators wish to participate. Yet, in many respects, baseball is a challenging game to watch. Because of the size of the ball, the rapidity and context dependence of the significant plays, and the absence of forward team progress across a field, it is a much less legible sport than, say, basketball or soccer, both of which can be followed more easily without commentary. Play-by-play announcers and commentators are as prominent and critical on television as on radio, and the legendary voices of the game—such as Vin Scully and Harry

Figure 9.1 Bobby Thomson rounds the bases following his game-ending three-run homer in the decisive finale of the 1951 playoff between the New York Giants and the Brooklyn Dodgers. Canonized by New York newspapers as "The Shot Heard 'Round the World," the home run would be commemorated over the ensuing decades by journalists, scholars, and novelists for its dramatic singularity—"the most vivid single moment, the grand exclamation point, in the history of the pastime." It was an event experienced simultaneously by millions of listeners and viewers. Radio stations in the United States had doubled between 1945 and 1950, and television sales were booming, spurred in large part by interest in watching baseball. This playoff series was in fact the first nationally televised sporting event in American history. *Bettmann/Getty Images*

Caray in the United States and Felo Ramirez in multiple Caribbean leagues—worked in both media. The task of providing radio commentary entails a bit more description, since listeners have less of a sense of where the ball is. (This is why Supreme Court Justice Sonia Sotomayor has recommended that new fans wishing to learn more about baseball listen to radio play-by-plays while watching the muted telecast.)[5] But television announcers also need to supply information that is not provided on screen, and even seasoned fans rely on sportscaster commentary.

At the ballpark itself, where official vocal commentary is limited to brief announcements of player names, large scoreboards perform the task of explicating the game. Scoreboard screens at high-level professional leagues in most countries do more than simply indicate who is winning. They count balls and strikes, track pitch velocity, announce official rulings about hits and errors, provide detailed player statistics, and generally supply information that is otherwise invisible to spectators but is often crucial for making sense of the action. The conspicuous role of the massive stadium scoreboard, introduced in the 1960s at Houston's Astrodome, complicates any distinction one might make between viewing a live baseball game and watching it on screen.

Scoreboards are central to the spectacle of baseball in other ways too. Since the introduction of instant replay displays in the 1970s (the technology had appeared on televised sports broadcasts, but not in stadiums, a decade earlier), much game-watching at the ballpark, especially consequential and visually compelling plays, takes place on the big screen after those plays have already occurred on the field. Interestingly, instant replay has become part of the game itself: most professional leagues use it to review and adjudicate important judgment calls by umpires. The common observation or lament that baseball is a hard sell to younger fans accustomed to consuming entertainment asynchronously on their devices is hard to square with the fact that much of the experience of the game, even at the stadium, involves asynchronous screen viewing.

As stadium scoreboards mediate the spectacle on the field for fans in the seats, they also provide other kinds of entertainment. From the days of Sportsman's Park in St. Louis in the nineteenth century, baseball teams have sought to engage spectators through diversions other than baseball. Twenty-first-century scoreboards present fans with such spectacles as dot racing, introduced in the 1980s in minor league games in Oklahoma City, in which lights simulate a race (a device that appeared decades prior in outdoor electric advertising on New York's Broadway[6]) that fans can follow, cheer, and privately wager on. Alternatively, the scoreboard and public announcement system will direct attention to the field or its periphery, where mascots or other costumed figures engage in races of their own and fans are called upon to perform challenging tasks, or to the stands where fans try to answer trivia questions. Summoning fans onto the field between innings to compete for prizes became a common feature of U.S. minor league entertainment during its resurgence as popular entertainment in the wake of the acclaimed 1988 film *Bull Durham*. But in MLB, as in Japan, it is typically the scoreboard that turns spectators into spectacle—through frequent video streams of fans cheering, dancing, kissing, or otherwise competing for the attention that will give them time on the big screen.

The one major baseball culture that forgoes these theatrical displays and game mediations is that in Cuba, where the sport remains preeminently popular, but as amateur competition, and where no capitalist enterprise seeks to maximize ticket sales, food and beverage purchases, or merchandise revenue. One might interpret the enduring appeal of Cuban baseball as evidence that the sport doesn't need pageantry and flashing lights to attract spectator interest. Arguably, however, the spectacular elements of game presentation in Japan, the United States, and other parts of the Caribbean are fundamental to the thing we call baseball, whereas Cuba's alternative path offers an interesting variant.

Regardless of which interpretation is favored, the fact remains that in most times and places, following a baseball game has not been limited to the ballpark, and ballpark entertainment has not been limited to following the game on the field. A stadium in which spectators are guessing the paid attendance, doing the wave, showing off dance moves for the camera, or (as in certain Japanese ballparks) releasing balloons into the air or waving miniature umbrellas is recognizable as a modern entertainment venue. And a media landscape in which distant fans stream games on their phones or crunch numbers tendentiously on fan websites has not changed the basic patterns of modern sports spectatorship.

10

Partisanship

Several years ago, Matt Casbolt, who now runs a fan account for the Baltimore Orioles out of Great Britain on a popular social media platform, picked his favorite baseball team out of a hat. An expatriate South African living in Sheffield, Casbolt discovered baseball at a minor league stadium while vacationing in the United States and began watching broadcasts upon his return home. As his interest in the sport intensified, he recognized the value of having a team to support. Casbolt wrote the names of all thirty major league franchises on slips of paper and then suffered the (short-term) misfortune of drawing a team with a long recent history of frustration. The Orioles' perennial failure to compete did not dampen Casbolt's enthusiasm, however, nor did it slow the growth of the team's substantial British fan base—long before the team's fortunes improved.

By some measure, Casbolt's ritual selection of the Orioles was an instant and automatic success. Although he had fallen in love with the sport as a minor league spectator, he understood that to truly qualify as a baseball fan, he needed to designate one big-league team as an object of selective interest and intense emotional investment. By declaring himself a supporter of a single club, he transformed himself from a baseball enthusiast to a partisan.

Baseball fandom can entail different kinds of engagement. As with most sports, a baseball fan might be someone who enjoys watching or discussing the game in all its dimensions and manifestations, no matter who is playing or what the stakes. Such fans might appreciate their chosen spectacle and follow its history in the same manner as opera afficionados, hip hop devotees, or news junkies. But the cultural appeal of baseball games over the years has not rested on that kind of consumer. Instead, baseball's status as mass entertainment, like that of many other team sports, has been sustained by fans who avow an interest in the outcomes of games and feel themselves implicated in those outcomes.

The most direct mechanism for enabling spectators to invest in contests in which they are not direct participants is a wager, and gambling has long facilitated fan interest in baseball, much as it has in soccer, boxing, or cockfighting in numerous societies. Betting on baseball thrives more than ever in the United States, most commonly in the form of fantasy games and online daily prediction contests conducted on internet sites such as Draft Kings. But this form of fan investment appears at the less visible margins of the sport, in part because of the taboos and vigilance that protect organized baseball from apparent threats of corruption and game-fixing. Just as important, the wagering interests of individuals don't create the fan communities that boost the appeal of team sports and often occupy center stage at the game itself.

Rather than betting, the classic act of fan engagement in team sports is rooting. Stereotypically, rooting is highly visible, audible, or performative (cheering, booing, chanting, dressing up), but it can also take the form of private acts of simply caring. In either mode, spectators respond to action on the baseball field as something that matters, generally because they prefer one team over another and most frequently because they feel a primary partisan allegiance to the team for which they root.

This dynamic is not unique to baseball. More famously, supporters of soccer teams in various parts of the world serve as paragons of partisan fandom. But baseball has some claims to historical primacy. The slang term *fan* originated as an Americanism in the 1890s, used first in print to describe and mock baseball spectators for their rooting practices. The word suggested fanatical devotion, but it also derived from an earlier English phrase, *the fancy*, denoting those who preferred (fancied) one side in a competition.

In the United States and in societies where baseball is the national sport (Cuba, Japan, and the Dominican Republic), baseball was the first team sport to cultivate this kind of preferential spectatorial engagement. Thus, it provided models for the modern experience of feeling included in a mass entertainment spectacle by virtue of feeling implicated in the success or failure of a sports team.

Unlike Matt Casbolt, whose selection unfolded in solitude, most sports fans forge allegiances to their team collectively, sometimes in a moment of affinity with a roaring crowd, more often after prolonged and repeated exposure to the habits and rituals of friends, siblings, and neighbors. Among fans who get called diehard, typically because their support and enthusiasm survive their own geographical relocation and extended periods of team failure, the allegiance often presents as a family heirloom, bequeathed from a parent or grandparent and perhaps shared among a cohort of heirs and successors.

Among both deeply devoted and casually attached fans, baseball's partisan allegiances tend to be based on and reinforced by geographical proximity. This has been especially true in the United States, where professional leagues granted territorial monopolies to their original members and clubs have been at least nominally identified with specific cities. Rooting for the home team was a standard norm in American baseball, long before "Take Me Out to the Ballgame" canonized the injunction, due largely to access to ballparks and local news. In the middle third of the century, radio broadcasts expanded these homelands, creating Venn diagrams of overlapping exposure to distant clubs, but geographical partisanship did not wane in the process. Fans in parts of the Midwest enjoyed comparably strong signals from WGN in Chicago and KMOX in St. Louis (and their many affiliated stations), for example, yet fan preferences still tended to correlate with latitude. To this day, one can trace the borders separating Cub country from Cardinal country in central Illinois. Cable television superstations in the 1980s briefly unsettled the map, allowing distant viewers to form attachments to teams from Atlanta and Chicago. But the segmentation of regional media markets largely persisted, and even in an era when games can be streamed on apps across oceans, such that a supporter in Sheffield can stay up late to catch home games in Baltimore, surveys of rooting in Major League Baseball consistently reveal overwhelming preferences for the team that plays closest to home.

In other, geographically smaller countries such as Japan and the Dominican Republic, where more teams cluster in the same metropolitan areas, this pattern is weaker, and affinities based on class, culture, subculture, politics, or regional identity may contribute more conspicuously to partisan affiliations. The major Dominican rivalry pits two teams from the capital with strong fan bases throughout the country that don't divide along geographical lines and are deeply rooted in a history that includes an extended chapter in which one of the clubs (the Leones of Escogido) was sponsored by dictator Rafael Trujillo. Japan's immensely popular Hanshin Tigers have long played in proximity to multiple other teams in the Kansai region, but the Tigers alone appear to benefit from regional chauvinism. At the same time, Hanshin boasts a sprawling network of official fan organizations located in every part of the archipelago, as far from home as Okinawa and Hokkaido (Figure 10.1).

Even in the United States, geography cannot fully explain fan allegiance, especially in areas with two home teams. In the first half of the twentieth century, most teams in the American League shared a home city with a National League club, though the paired teams rarely faced each other. In the post–World War II era, however, three of those cities (Boston, St. Louis, and Philadelphia) saw one of their franchises relocate, leaving a single local club, and the teams that shared New York found themselves squaring off in the World Series with great frequency. In fact, during this period, New York housed three teams—the Yankees, Giants, and Dodgers—and although they played in different boroughs, their respective

Figure 10.1 Members of the Chunichi Dragons ōendan in Nagoya, Japan, rally the home crowd. Ōendans (cheering sections), featuring taiko drums and brass instruments, form a major part of the stadium experience at Japanese baseball games. Caribbean baseball fans (unlike those in North America) also play music while their favored team is at bat, but an ōendan is a formally organized club, often with an elaborate governing structure and a potentially delicate or tense relationship with the corporation that owns the team that it is supporting. *Brett Bull/The Tokyo Reporter*

fan communities divided along lines that were not simply about residential location. Writing in 1962, a few years after two of the clubs had decamped to California, journalist Murray Kempton offered a taxonomy that recaptured (tendentiously) the fault lines of partisan affiliation, or at least some of the conceits of partisan identity: "The old Dodger fans were the kind of people who picket. The old Giant fans would be embarrassed to do anything so conspicuous, but they were the kind of people who refuse to cross picket lines. Yankee fans are the kind of people who think they own the company the picket line is thrown around."

A more straightforward consideration in fan preference and allegiance is success. As in other team sports, die-hard supporters of a baseball club deride bandwagon or fair-weather fans and take special pride in their own loyalty to a losing cause. In a fan memoir based on his lifelong experience rooting for the University of Michigan football team, law professor Paul Campos argues that suffering through losses is the point—the cathartic fulfillment—of partisan fandom. But for most fans, it's winning that cements the bonds. Successful teams have as a rule drawn more spectators, both in the stadium and on the screen, and perennially dominant franchises that win repeated championships, such as Japan's Yomiuri Giants, Los Tigres del Licey in the Dominican League, and the New York Yankees, enjoy the largest fan bases in their countries. Partisans of other teams, including the Boston Red Sox, the Chicago Cubs, and the Hanshin Tigers, have historically worn their teams' shortfalls as badges of honor, but when those franchises turned things around and ended their championship droughts, attendance rose even higher and devoted fans had little trouble adjusting to success.

In the world of team sports, individual athletes rarely anchor enduring fan preferences. This is especially true in baseball, where the impact of a single performer on the average game's outcome tends to be lower. At least nine different figures are given equal opportunities to score (more than in basketball and soccer), and unlike in American football the player with the most significant impact on the game (the starting pitcher) appears in no more than one in five games. A fan might watch an NBA game primarily to see the hometown superstar, but in baseball that would be a recipe for disappointment. Partisan spectators often have a favorite player, but their attachment to the team typically survives that player's likely departure or inevitable retirement.

Whereas many models of fandom, especially in popular music or cinema, presuppose an imagined identification between an individual spectator and a celebrity figure, partisan baseball fans indulge a different kind of fantasy: that of team membership. Official merchandise blurs the lines between the athletes and spectators. Fans wear uniforms with players' names and numbers emblazoned on the back, and players reciprocate, after a fashion; their outfits are often indistinguishable from those in the stands, and they typically foreground the collective identity of the franchise or the city. The children (or adults) in the bleachers or at home wearing a Los Angeles Angels jersey bearing Mike Trout's name, or their own, are easily misread as wishing or pretending to be a fabulously talented athlete. One might instead (and more sympathetically) see them as suiting up for their team's game. Not everyone in the Angels' organization, or even everyone sitting in the dugout wearing the official jersey, can hit a curveball or run to first base without panting. Yet they are still members of the team. And in some sense so too are their loyal partisans.

Uniforms stand prominently for club membership in baseball, which is the only major team sport in which coaches and managers dress like players. Uniforms can also bestow continuity on the otherwise elusive entity that fans are rooting for, given how frequently rosters turn over. Exceptional players who remain with the same organization for an entire career become objects of veneration in part because their loyalty mirrors that of their supporters. Under these circumstances, the comedian Jerry Seinfeld famously observed, fans are essentially rooting for laundry. But even uniforms change and vary; most MLB teams now sport multiple uniform designs over the course of a single season. Stadium locations change too, and so do team names occasionally. Few fans in Orange County switched or severed allegiances when the California Angels retitled themselves the Anaheim Angels and then later the Los Angeles Angels of Anaheim. The same goes for transfers of team ownership. So perhaps fans are in the compromised position of rooting for nothing more than a corporation.

Yet when a franchise relocates to a distant city, the ties that bind its fans are tested, raising the possibility that a team's claim to represent a place might be necessary (though not sufficient) to its continuous identity. Occasionally fans have followed their team (emotionally speaking) to a new home, but more often the move is experienced as a deep betrayal, exposing the fault line that had always separated the fan base from the franchise's suddenly vilified owner. Fans often openly resent the person or group in the owner's box, not only because the parsimony of the business constrains the team's success on the field by limiting payroll, and not only because owners get rich at the direct expense of spectators, but also because owners are partisan fans' bitter rivals for the claim to possess the team. The tension embedded in this rivalry explodes into open warfare whenever owners try to assert their power by taking the team elsewhere. Amidst longstanding and ultimately accurate reports that the Oakland Athletics would be leaving the Bay Area, the dwindling crowds at the ballpark in 2024 regularly erupted in chants of "Sell the Team!"

Fantasies of owning or belonging to a baseball team suffuse the larger ritualized culture of partisan fandom. Lucky jerseys, auspiciously positioned caps, painfully averted gazes, strategically muted televisions, and countless other attempts to produce fortune on the field are all familiar fan gestures. Classic baseball movies register and reinforce this kind of magical thinking, especially about the impact that an individual invested spectator's attention might have on the outcome. Even the *Moneyball* film (though not the book on which it was based), which is ostensibly dedicated to showing that baseball is a game of rationality, probability, and predictability, portrays its protagonist executive as superstitiously refusing to attend his team's games during a winning streak. Though Billy Beane's habitual absence from Oakland's games was in fact an attempt to manage anxiety about the limits of his control over the team's fate, the cinematic version of his story transmuted that concern into its exact opposite—the intuition that his own conduct as a spectator actually *did* affect that fate.

This intuition, shared by many partisan supporters of sports teams, probably reinforces the movie industry's own preoccupations with visual attention, but it extends far beyond the act of watching. Nor is it unique to baseball or even to sports. Caring about an outcome of public interest over which one has little or no control may be an especially common predicament in modern mass consumer culture (and mass politics), and it also fits broader habits of magical thinking and religious piety. In imagining that their actions and even their mental states are part of the contest on the field, baseball fans tap into primal human tendencies to ascribe omnipotence to one's own thoughts, on the one hand, and to bow before unseen powers, on the other.

Unseen powers loom large in baseball. Fan websites speak often of the gods of baseball, who sometimes represent randomness and caprice, but can also stand for justice. When they are supporters of a team, and not simply enthusiasts of a sport, baseball fans must take special care not to offend those deities. In his study of the choreographed cheering of Japanese baseball fan clubs, sociologist Hidesato Takahashi has observed that those stadium chants share the distinctive rhythmic patterns of medieval agricultural songs directed to the divine, so that even when an encouraging cheer is addressed (nominally and grammatically) to the player at bat, the real intended audience lies elsewhere. Other scholars highlight the role of fan exhortations as bids to take part in the efforts they are exhorting and to "participate in the spectacle on display of which their teams' performance is only a part."[1] But the anguished, earnest, or ecstatic expressions on the faces of fans as they await one of the innumerable moments in a baseball game when it appears that anything (or nothing) is about to happen suggest something beyond the impulse of spectators to blur the lines between audience and performer. They suggest instead the helplessness and hopefulness of the supplicant.

11

Accounting

In 2024, Major League Baseball announced that Ty Cobb, almost a century after his retirement and more than five decades after his death, was no longer the career recordholder for batting average, a distinction often translated as his being baseball's all-time leading hitter. Josh Gibson, the man who broke his record, had been deceased far longer than Cobb. What changed was a league ruling that acknowledged the official status of regular-season at-bats in the major Negro Leagues, where Gibson played for most of his professional career, amassing a .372 batting average, six points higher than Cobb's figure, which had stood for decades and seemed likely never to be surpassed.

This statistical correction was not simply a matter of geeky curiosity. Or rather, the fact that it most certainly is a matter of geeky curiosity did not make it a marginal affair to the world of U.S. baseball, did not prevent Gibson's coronation from headlining the MLB website for several days, and did not limit fan interest (or the sparks of outrage on comment boards and social media, including a Facebook group from which Ty Cobb's granddaughter was exiled as a "nitwit loser who was willing to support giving away Cobb's hard-earned titles due to Wokeness"[1]). Despite the fact that Cobb, Gibson, all their teammates, and practically every spectator who witnessed either of them play were long dead, and despite the total absence of financial stakes attached to the record, the correction made news because baseball is, famously, a game of statistics.

What that means, however, is a subject of disagreement and confusion. An obsession with precise statistics has characterized the sport since its inception and is often cited as central to its appeal or as a barrier to entry, even though statistical recordkeeping would seem to be a feature of all modern spectator sports—and most modern political, economic, and social institutions. At the same time, the techniques and discourse of statistical analysis employed today in baseball are often held up as the clearest evidence that the sport has fundamentally changed.

Baseball's culture of obsessive statistical reckoning combines several related elements, none of which is unique among modern team spectator sports, but all of which have been intensified in the case of baseball by the game's structure and the sport's history. First is an interest in evaluating and crediting the contributions of individual players to a team's success or failure. Second is an extraordinary faith in the capacity of numbers to precisely and reliably summarize important events. And third is a need to tell stories about a game in a language that allows for comparing events spread across time.

The careful recording and tabulating of events within a baseball game, including events that don't directly determine or explain the game's outcome, has been around ever since the game became a subject of news coverage. Meticulous baseball statistics, in other words, are as old as the spectator sport of baseball. From its infancy, this culture of recording and tabulation bore the heavy imprint of one man, Henry Chadwick, who moved from England to New York with his family at age twelve in the 1830s. After working as a cricket reporter, Chadwick took an interest in local baseball games in the 1850s and became one of the new sport's leading boosters. As a reporter for New York papers, and then as the editor of official baseball guides, Chadwick cultivated fan interest in (and reverence for) recordkeeping, while also shaping the kinds of statistics that were kept and valued.

Even before Chadwick appeared on the scene around midcentury, baseball clubs had committed themselves to basic accounting. By-laws of clubs playing various versions of baseball in the 1830s and 1840s stipulated that game results needed to be recorded, along with the exact score and the names of players. Already in 1845 a numerical game record—labeled an "abstract"—appeared in a New York daily. But Chadwick radically expanded and significantly standardized the way baseball games were abstracted and thereby understood. He introduced the box score, featuring a column for player names and their individual performances, as well as a line score showing the number of runs tallied by each team in each inning. Chadwick also developed a code for specifying the outcome of each at-bat, which he used for his own notes but encouraged others to emulate. The persistent and widespread practice of individual fans scoring by hand in private documents (ideally redundant with the public record), which has no parallel among spectator sports, has perpetuated Chadwick's tradition, including his idiosyncratic choice of the letter K to represent a strikeout.

Baseball's accounting practices emerged in a period of widespread numeracy in the United States and increasing use of quantitative analysis by bureaucratic states in the Western world. Still, Chadwick's box score and scorecards reflected more specific influences and ideologies. In his evangelical pursuit of statistics, Chadwick was acting on several articles of the faith that animated middle-class reformers of the era. Like his older half-brother, Sir Edwin Chadwick, who was Britain's Commissioner of the Board of Health and the architect of its Poor Law reformation, Henry Chadwick believed in data collection as the foundation for a scientific approach to social disorder. For baseball to fulfill its mission as "moral recreation," exhaustive and accurate statistics were necessary. Moreover, those statistics needed to illuminate the role of the individual, not just the team. Although middle-class reformers in midcentury America promoted group activities and organizations (temperance societies, fraternal orders, and other voluntary associations), they stressed individual accountability and saw the self as the site and target of their reform efforts. Thus, while baseball was a collective enterprise requiring collaboration and camaraderie, credit or blame for success and failure belonged to individuals as well. Fans needed to know which players had done well—or poorly.

Early baseball recordkeeping focused on the runs and outs made by each player because these were the results that had been listed in cricket box scores. But the rules of baseball allow for a more varied set of batting outcomes. Whereas in cricket a hit automatically equals a run, baseball batters can hit safely but be subsequently retired on the basepaths or stranded on base at the end of an inning. They can also achieve a base safely without getting a hit—via a base on balls, a fielding error, getting hit by a pitch, or a fielder's choice to retire a runner at a different base. In 1859 Chadwick began producing complex box scores that listed hits and runs separately, while also registering the defensive performances of individual players, crediting them for assists and putouts, and holding them accountable for errors. Pitching was generally of minor concern.

Over the years, Chadwick tinkered with his categories, as did the rules committees of professional leagues (not always with his blessing), and pitching performance eventually assumed much greater significance. Still, Chadwick's ideological approach to baseball shaped basic patterns of baseball recordkeeping that became entrenched by the end of the nineteenth century. In addition to commitment to exhaustive documentation of each at-bat, crediting and blaming individual players, and the general emphasis on cumulative data, Chadwick's world view bequeathed specific legacies to baseball's statistical discourse. His distinction between earned and unearned runs (originally applied to batters but ultimately diverted to pitchers) and his interest in calculating averages shaped how the game was followed and became central components of fan engagement. Chadwick's legacy would also survive in a longstanding tendency among sportswriters, fans, and players to value the base hit as the game's fundamental offensive achievement, implicitly depreciating the significance of a walk (base on balls) and downplaying the consequential question of whether hits were singles, doubles, triples, or home runs. Chadwick especially disliked the home run, out of an interest in the interplay between hitters and fielders and an aesthetic preference for the sequences of run-producing hits and sacrifices that would later be called "small ball." He objected to the homer's brutal simplicity, though it might also have transgressed the protocols of male bodily control and moderation with which middle-class reform culture was preoccupied. Chadwick once expressed the odd concern that a home run would entail a "costly expenditure of physical strength" in running the full circuit of bases at once.[2]

One artifact of these various dispositions and prejudices was the dominance of the batting average in twentieth-century baseball statistics. A batting average represents the number of base hits batters achieve as a fraction of their plate appearances, while excluding from the denominator those plate appearances when a batter either receives a free base or sacrifices himself (under certain conditions recognized by the official scorer) to advance a runner. The fraction is then expressed, not as a percentage, but out of one thousand, so that a hitter who gets thirty base hits over a span of one hundred official at-bats is credited with a batting average of .300, which in turn is called three hundred and recognized as reaching a threshold of excellence. Chadwick did not invent this statistic, but he championed it, since, in addition to his fondness for arithmetic, it reflected his disdain for getting on base without a hit and his relative indifference to the magnitude of that hit. Walks added nothing to one's batting average, and the same value was assigned to a single as to a home run.

The batting average has always had detractors and was never the sole standard for assessing offensive value, but it played an outsized role in determining player compensation and especially in the awarding of three high-profile distinctions that MLB created in the 1930s: the Most Valuable Player award, selection to an All-Star game, and induction into the Hall of Fame. It also provided the only contribution of baseball's statistical vocabulary (as distinct from terms or expressions that describe features of the game itself, such as *home run, out of left field,* or *getting to first base*) to idiomatic U.S. English. Americans who speak of *batting a thousand* to denote a 100 percent success rate invoke a thousand-point scale that makes sense only to those exposed, directly or indirectly, to baseball statistics. Caribbean and Asian leagues also calculate, display, and compare batting averages, making Chadwick's favored statistical measure an enduring feature of global baseball.

Even in the twenty-first century, when analysts downplay its significance, batting average remains the leading category in baseball's statistical landscape. It is the most prominent figure on a player's baseball card or scoreboard listing. And among all the record book modifications necessitated by the inclusion of Negro League statistics, the posthumous acknowledgment of Josh Gibson's career-high batting average topped the headlines. Perhaps most intriguingly, fans' emphasis on batting average has contributed to the oft-repeated observation that baseball is a game of failure, since even superstars bat below .333 and thus succeed less than a third of the time. It's a questionable insight that says less about the game than about the statistical category. If we measured batters by how often they reach base in a single game or by the proportion of their swings that make contact, we would draw very different conclusions about the sport's relationship to success and failure, much as we would if we focused on pitchers rather than hitters. But because batting average reigns supreme, clichés about the humbling nature of baseball persist.

And yet batting average is only one of many metrics over which fans, club management, and players themselves have long obsessed, which is why baseball enjoys a reputation for statistical entertainment. Throughout the twentieth century, following baseball meant tracking the total number of home runs, runs scored, runs batted in, and stolen bases of individual batters, the earned run averages, strikeouts, and win–loss records of individual pitchers—and the definitions of those terms. By century's end, a vast menu of statistics appeared in newspapers and broadcasts and on the backs of trading cards: fielding percentage (the number of errorless plays as a proportion of total opportunities), total bases, slugging percentage (total bases divided by at-bats), on-base average (hits, walks, and times hit-by-pitch divided by at-bats), game-winning runs batted in, innings pitched, complete games, and relief pitchers' saves. In more recent decades, avid fans have had to master still dozens more figures and acronyms.

This proliferation of statistical categories and vocabulary marks baseball as more oriented around numbers and recordkeeping than any other sport. The distinction may reflect the range of formally discrete and countable components of a scoring opportunity. This is in contrast with hockey, lacrosse, and soccer, for example, where scoring takes a single form, actions setting up a score are less clearly bounded or defined, and the game flow inhibits analysis of individual plays. It may also reflect the unusual role of pitching among defensive actions in both baseball and other sports.

But the most striking difference in baseball statistics lies in the extent to which they depend on judgments by someone other than a referee. All team sports require on-field judgment calls: is a player in bounds, is a play offsides, did the puck cross the crease of a net, is a bodily collision a foul, does conduct warrant ejection, is a pitch a strike? But most of baseball's storied stats depend as well on the opinions of official scorers (should a fielder have caught a well-struck ball, would a run have scored without an error, was a pitch that got loose the fault of the pitcher or the catcher?) and are subject to complex rules that are worked out far from the field by people who don't suit up for the game (Figure 11.1).

With a couple of glaring exceptions (most prominently the Chadwick-invented category of pitchers' wins and losses, which credits a single pitcher for a team victory and penalizes a single

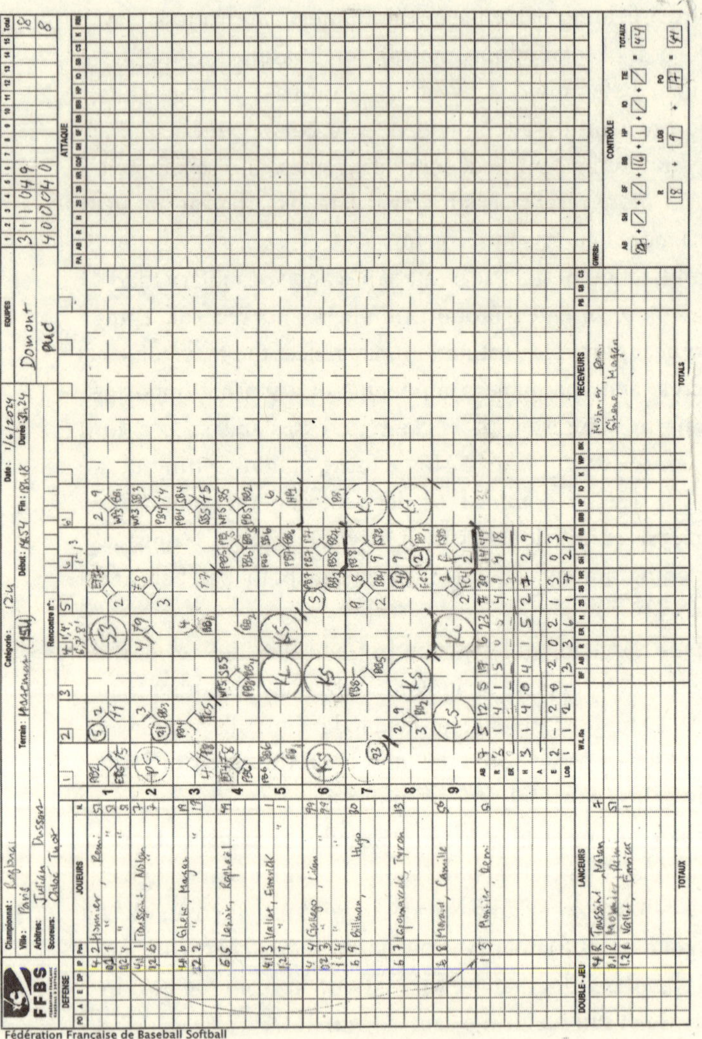

Figure 11.1 A scorecard from a Paris U-12 game in 2024 meticulously documents every event in a game played by pre-teens. As in many little leagues, this game was played under rules that deviate from that of MLB and are not subject to its jurisdiction. Few of the children playing in games follow professional baseball, and most don't speak English, Japanese, or Spanish. Yet what links this competition to the larger history of organized baseball is the fact that each at-bat in every game gets scored in methods and shorthand derived from longstanding U.S. practices. *Photo courtesy of Chloé Tuot*

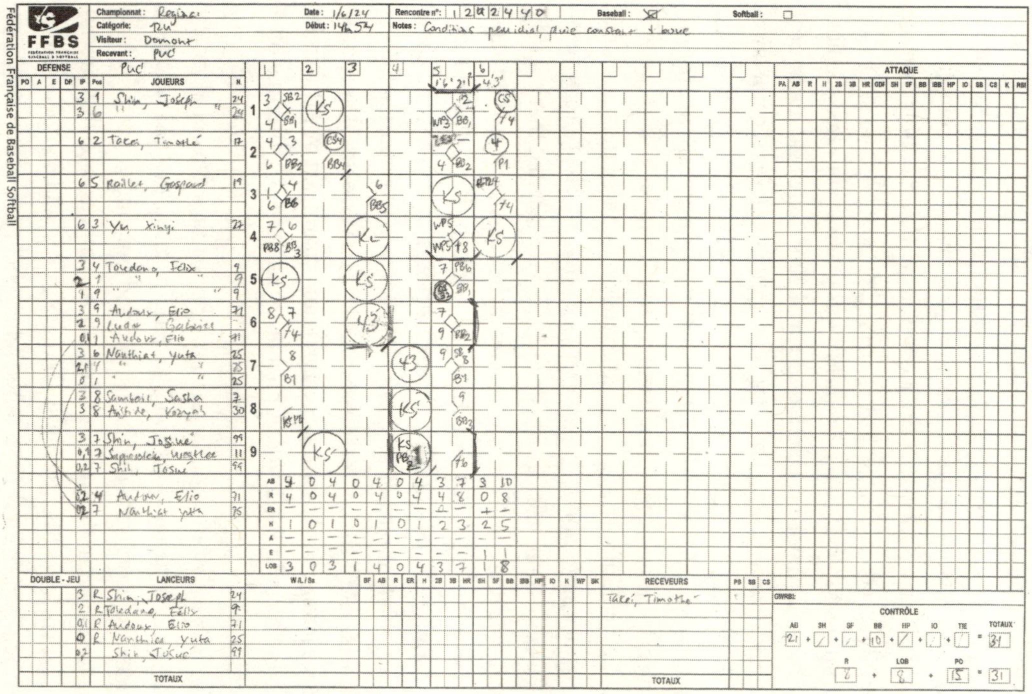

Figure 11.1 *Continued*

pitcher for the defeat), baseball's legacy statistics don't tell clear stories about the main question that animates fans and bettors, which is whether a favored team prevailed. But despite not reflecting outcomes, individual statistics have long affected how the game is played, even in ways oblique or contrary to their strategic value. For more than a century, fans and journalists have complained about players prioritizing their quest for a higher batting average over the needs of the team or altering their play with an eye to the record books. In 1910, St. Louis Browns pitchers appeared to allow Cleveland's Napoleon Lajoie to get base hits so that he might beat out the detested Ty Cobb for the batting title—a competition heightened by a prize of a new car—much as the Yomiuri Giants intentionally walked Randy Bass in 1985, against team interest, to protect their manager's longstanding home run record.

More commonly, statistical idiosyncrasies have affected managerial decisions about when to replace pitchers. The rules governing win–loss records, which since 1950 have dictated that starting pitchers get credit for the win only if they complete five innings, motivate both pitcher and manager to reach that threshold and discourage the potentially advisable strategy of opening the game with a different pitcher for the first time facing an opposing lineup. More bizarre is the controversial category of saves, defined by sportswriter Jerome Holtzman in the 1960s and canonized by MLB in its current form in the 1970s. A pitcher earns a save by finishing off a victory, but only under a set of quite specific circumstances. In part because of the drama surrounding the final outs of a contest that has no game clock, and in part because the task allows a pitcher to throw as hard as possible without worrying about having to remain in the game for long, certain pitchers (called *closers*) specialize in getting these outs and are valued and compensated at a much higher level than other relief pitchers—largely based on their save totals. Managers are reluctant to employ them in "nonsave situations" and are criticized for doing so, even though the distinction between situations can seem arbitrary and despite the fact that the closer might be better used earlier against more dangerous hitters. Strikingly, many closers appear uncomfortable outside of the role established by the narrow parameters of the save rule. Statistical variables are regulated from beyond the ballpark, but they are never far from the minds of those on the field.

Despite obsessive vigilance, professional baseball's recordkeeping regime has been contested, malleable, and sometimes fragile. One area of instability concerns the question of all-time records. The 2024 dethroning of Ty Cobb as baseball's batting leader is only the most recent such revision. Sometimes the uncertainty has revolved around the question of whether to use the accounting procedures at the time of the event (for example, when walks counted as hits, when starting pitchers did not need to finish the fifth inning to qualify for a win, or when a game-ending hit over the fence didn't count as a home run unless that run was necessary to end the game) or whether later policies ought to be applied retroactively.

Baseball record books, which until the 1990s were compiled by private publishers and were not subject to the authority of the league, also had to decide how to account for the fact that baseball seasons were once shorter. In 1961 Roger Maris eclipsed Babe Ruth's single-season record of sixty home runs, but because he accomplished the feat in a 162-game season (Ruth's seasons lasted only 154 games), many in the sport, including Commissioner Ford Frick, sought to preserve Ruth's mark. Some record books listed both players with their respective home run totals and season lengths, and one journalist advocated placing an asterisk alongside Maris's new record—though that did not happen.

If determining recordholders has proven challenging, determining the statistical record itself has posed more basic problems. Over the years, as errors or lacunae in the records of official scorers and box scores have been discovered, statistical achievements have been added or subtracted retroactively. Babe Ruth's career mark for runs batted in was revised upwards by two as the result of an earlier clerical error, though Hank Aaron would soon thereafter exceed both figures. In 1977 a researcher detected a miscrediting of a player driving in a run forty-seven years earlier. Its official correction not only restored integrity to the record books, but also meant that Hack Wilson's single-season RBI record now stood slightly further out of reach, at 191 rather than 190. Many journalists and league officials resisted the corrective project, especially when it threatened to alter records long cherished by fans. Statistical lore, they rightly observed, was part of the game itself. To them, *a record* in the *Guinness Book* sense of the term was as important as *the record* in the archival or stenographic sense. On the other side of the debate, a chorus of outsiders disagreed and ultimately prevailed. As John Thorn, baseball's preeminent historian and a leading figure in the quest for accurate accounting, declared: "there can be *no statute of limitations* on historical error."[3]

Discrepancies might seem surprising in a game that values meticulous recordkeeping, or perhaps they remind us of the impossibility of ensuring accuracy in the age before video recordings. But it is remarkable nonetheless how well documented baseball games were. We have more detailed, exhaustive, and reliable information about what happened on baseball fields over a century ago than about any other aspect of leisure culture, popular entertainment, or daily life in the United States from that era. It is equally noteworthy that baseball has attracted armies of entrepreneurs and volunteer researchers over the intervening decades who devoted their lives to correcting, curating, and interpreting that historical record.

Supplemented by radio recordings and film, professional baseball's more recent history, especially in North America, is less subject to revision. And in the age of smartphones and personal computers, the sport's full statistical record is easily accessed. Within seconds of wondering, fans or historians can authoritatively answer the question of what happened in the third inning of a game played in 1933 or the lifetime WHIP (walks and hits per inning pitched) of Mordecai "Three Fingers" Brown. The solidity of the digital archive is the product of decades of painstaking tabulation and research, culminating in the 1960s with the compilation and publication of *The Baseball Encyclopedia* (1969), which reconstructed game box scores dating back to 1876 and used computerized punch cards to aggregate and arrange data for over 10,000 major league players. The finished project, which ran to 2,338 pages, corrected numerous statistical errors in previous official publications and provided a foundation for the electronic resources that fans rely upon today, though the encyclopedia itself was displaced in 1989 by the even more thorough and reliable *Total Baseball*, which soon became the sport's official record book.

The 1969 publication also launched professional baseball's digital age, which is often marked by the founding (in Cooperstown) of the Society for American Baseball Research (SABR), dedicated to using computers and statistics for understanding the sport's history and producing what data guru Bill James called "objective knowledge about baseball." More generally, the SABR acronym and the derived term *sabermetrics* dominate the common narrative that baseball has been fundamentally transformed by new techniques of statistical analysis. This view, popularized by the book *Moneyball* (2003) and its movie adaptation (2011), generally locates the change around the beginning of the current century, when new statistical categories and new ideas about game strategy and player value swept away ancient pieties and revolutionized the sport.[4]

In some respects, these changes are glaringly evident. Persuaded by statistical analysis of the higher cost of outs, for example, professional teams (even in Japan) are now less likely to bunt or attempt a stolen base in order to advance a runner. And armed with more detailed information about the tendencies of each batter, teams reposition their fielders more frequently, dramatically, and effectively. The statistical revolution is even more obvious off the field, in the way commentators, managers, players, and fans discuss the game. Figures that were once arcane, such as slugging percentage and on-base average, now assume prominence, while an entirely new statistical vocabulary is suffusing baseball discourse in the twenty-first century. Fans speak casually of spin rates, launch angles, defensive runs saved, and the ambitiously comprehensive category of WAR (Wins Against Replacement), which measures players' contributions in terms of how many additional games their teams are likely to win with them, rather than a substitute at their position. In more data-savvy blogs and internet discussions, mathematical formulas are deployed confidently, and a panoply of new acronyms and symbols—wRC+, FIP, BABIP, CT%—are as transparent as ERA and RBI. The twenty-first-century statistical regime also operates behind the scenes: every MLB club now employs a data analytics department.

Nonetheless, talk of revolutionary change can be misleading. The *Moneyball* narrative overstates the novelty of the analytic turn in twenty-first-century baseball, misconstrues its significance, and overstates the role of computational technology in the genuinely new trends that shape the sport. Baseball has always been a game of numbers, averages, data, and probability. Recent trends in game strategy and player evaluation do not reflect a new statistical approach, ideology, or discovery. Throughout the twentieth century, statistically minded fans and journalists calculated the benefits and costs of managerial decisions, questioned the dominant statistical categories, and demonstrated with pen, paper, and mathematical formula most of the claims that underlie the ostensibly new insights of sabermetrics. Nor did they keep this knowledge to themselves; they published their arguments in scholarly journals and the sporting papers and appeared in mass media. A 1954 *Life* magazine article, titled "Goodby [sic] to Some Old Baseball Ideas," included a photo of a complex mathematical formula. Ten years later a *Sports Illustrated* article on the work of a different baseball statistician ran under the headline "Baseball Is

Played All Wrong." Philip Roth's *The Great American Novel* (1973) featured a wunderkind baseball strategist who had run all the numbers by age seven and had arrived at similar strategic conclusions: don't bunt, forgo intentional walks, put the best hitters earlier in the batting order.

This approach, now celebrated as "Smart Baseball," does not represent a recent intellectual or technological breakthrough. Instead, it reflects the adoption by professional clubs of strategic insights that had been around for decades but were until recently ignored by those who set rosters and called plays. Even the novelty of that development can be overstated. The Brooklyn Dodgers hired a full-time statistician in the 1940s, as part of another Branch Rickey initiative to modernize the game and maximize profits. A couple of the moves that Rickey made in the late 1940s that are usually understood in terms of racial politics, such as trading away segregationist Dixie Walker and moving Jackie Robinson into the hallowed fourth spot in the batting order, also reflected statistical insights about player performance produced by Rickey's numbers guy Allan Roth (no relation to the novelist), the man profiled in *Life* magazine.

The popular impression that until the twenty-first century, when the nerds had their revenge and the management consultants ascended to power, the business and pleasure of baseball were exclusively a matter of hunches, ineffable instincts, and superstitious beliefs ignores both this history and, more generally, fans' lifelong preoccupation with numbers and statistical averages. The introduction in 1951 of Topps Chewing Gum cards marks a milestone in that history, enlisting young children in the project of statistical comparison. Beginning around the same era, popular tabletop games used the statistical records of real players to set probabilistic parameters of their performance, allowing both children and adults to play at managing big-league teams. A game called National Pastime had introduced this model in 1930, and in 1941

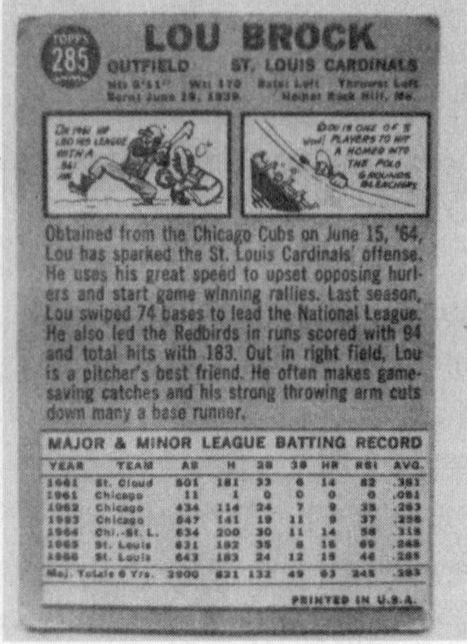

LOU BROCK

OUTFIELD   ST. LOUIS CARDINALS

Obtained from the Chicago Cubs on June 15, '64, Lou has sparked the St. Louis Cardinals' offense. He uses his great speed to upset opposing hurlers and start game winning rallies. Last season, Lou swiped 74 bases to lead the National League. He also led the Redbirds in runs scored with 94 and total hits with 183. Out in right field, Lou is a pitcher's best friend. He often makes game-saving catches and his strong throwing arm cuts down many a base runner.

MAJOR & MINOR LEAGUE BATTING RECORD							
YEAR	TEAM	AB	H	2B	3B	HR	RBI	AVG.
1961	St. Cloud	501	181	33	6	14	82	.361
1961	Chicago	11	1	0	0	0	0	.091
1962	Chicago	434	114	24	7	9	35	.263
1963	Chicago	547	141	19	11	9	37	.258
1964	Chi.-St. L.	634	200	30	11	14	58	.315
1965	St. Louis	631	182	35	8	16	69	.288
1966	St. Louis	643	183	24	12	15	46	.285
Maj. Totals 6 Yrs.		2900	821	132	49	63	245	.283

PRINTED IN U.S.A.

Figure 11.2 Hall of Famer Lou Brock, part of the first generation of Black ballplayers to grow up after the integration of Major League Baseball, appears on a typical Topps baseball card for 1967. Collectible sports cards had been sold and traded since the nineteenth century, but they mostly emphasized player likeness and celebrity. Topps cards, introduced in 1951, called attention instead to a player's detailed record across a range of categories over a career trajectory. *Photo from author's personal collection*

All-Star Baseball achieved commercial success. Twenty years later, Strat-O-Matic baseball featured dice, rather than a spinner, and added pitching statistics to the mix. It became (and remains) spectacularly profitable (Figure 11.2).

What distinguishes baseball's statistical culture in the twenty-first century, then, is not quantification, data science, or hard-headed probabilistic thinking. Apart from the ease and speed with which statistics can be accessed and authenticated, the most significant change lies in the ability of new technologies of video recording and spatial location to capture bats, balls, and bodies in motion. Whereas many favored sabermetric categories have been long available, and numbers like WAR can even be calculated retroactively for nineteenth-century players, spin rates of pitches and exit velocity of batted balls have only recently become measurable. Without precise tracking and timing of moving objects, new statistics like defensive runs saved (which assesses how the average fielder would have handled the same batted ball) and chase rates (which measures how often a hitter swings at a ball that is not in the strike zone) would not be reliable.

Freezing and measuring movement also helps players and coaches in developing swing mechanics, refining pitching motions, and determining defensive positioning. These technological advances have changed all professional sports, as high-definition video cameras and Doppler radar offer unprecedented perspectives on game action. What distinguishes baseball from, say, soccer, is that whereas soccer teams deploy these technologies proprietarily and protect most of the information they generate, MLB made the significant decision in 2015 to install Statcast devices in every ballpark and license their use to broadcasters. Data regarding the speed, acceleration, and trajectory of the ball are immediately reported to fans on their televisions or phones—and thus become part of the spectacle.

To sabermetric analysts, tracking balls, bats, and bodies has additional value because it isolates events over which players have more control. Numbers like exit velocity and vertical break don't tell us how a hit or a pitch figured in a game, but they give some indication of whether a batter struck the ball hard or whether a curveball had significant downward movement. And in the new statistical landscape, that's especially important because the focus of stats talk has shifted from the Chadwickian question of who deserves credit or blame for past action to the tasks of projecting future outcomes and commodifying present talent. Prominent new metrics like Fielding Independent Pitching and Batting Average on Balls in Play attempt to screen out what actually happened as just so much noise in order to focus on the events that are likely to have predictive value. And yet they find their place in baseball's older statistical culture because baseball fans, even the most traditionalist, have always shown an insatiable appetite for keeping the books.

12

Conclusion

Imagination and Fantasy

In his late twenties, Haruki Murakami ran a café and jazz club in Tokyo. On the opening day of the 1978 baseball season in Japan's Central League, he took the afternoon off to sit beyond the out-field fence at Jingu Stadium, where his beloved Yakult Swallows were hosting the Hiroshima Carp. Narrating the event with images and sentiments that fans often favor in their memoirs, he recalled: "The sky was a sparkling blue, the draft beer as cold as cold could be, and the ball strikingly white against the green field, the first green I had seen in a long time. To fully appreciate a baseball game, you really have to be there in person!" But what happened next was entirely unexpected. Swallows' leadoff hitter Dave Hilton struck double to left and Murakami experienced an epiphany: he would write a novel.

The connection between the hit and the sudden decision to become a writer goes as unexplained in Murakami's account as many of the uncanny convergences that appear in the novels he would publish over the next several decades. Murakami's fiction, which has made him an international bestseller and one of Japan's most eminent literary figures, rarely features Japan's national sport. But the prominence of baseball in the origin story of an author famous for magical realism is significant. And the connection between his baseball fandom and his fiction writing does not end on opening day. "Over the next six months or so that followed," Murakami relates, he wrote his first novel. "I wrapped up the first draft right when baseball season ended.

Incidentally, that year the Yakult Swallows bucked the odds and almost everyone's predictions to win the Central League pennant, then went on to…[win] the Japan Series. It was a glorious, miraculous season."[1]

In the imagination of many novelists and fans, baseball is indeed a land of miracles. Magical events are staples of baseball fiction, a phenomenon most familiar to North American readers in the works of W. P. Kinsella (*Shoeless Joe* and *The Iowa Baseball Confederacy*). More generally, baseball fans and commentators are renowned for invoking jinxes, curses, and talismans to explain what happens on the field, even as the sport proudly embraces data science.

Miracles, fate, and deities make for more poetic baseball writing, of course, and the abundant literary representations of the game in English, Japanese, and Spanish have tended to highlight and reinforce supernatural, imaginative, folkloric, or psychological dimensions and perspectives. Poets have been especially drawn to the sport. Even discounting those remembered primarily for popular light verse about baseball (Ernest Thayer and Franklin P. Adams), the list of eminent poets who found in baseball compelling subject matter is striking. Modernists Marianne Moore, William Carlos Williams, and May Swenson all produced baseball poetry, as did Robert Frost, Nicolás Guillén, Donald Hall, the humorist Ogden Nash, and the haiku poet Yotsuya Ryu.

It might be tempting to identify in baseball a split between the "Two Cultures" of science and humanities whose bifurcation the British writer C. P. Snow influentially lamented in 1959. But the divisions between scientific and literary, quantitative and verbal, or left-brain and right-brain approaches to baseball are misleading. They bear some resemblance to the inaccurate portrait peddled by recent Hollywood movies of baseball talent evaluation, which pits the number crunchers and bean counters against scouts who can hear the break of a curveball with their eyes closed and can foretell a player's prospects by instinct. Much as scouts have always combined intuitive judgment and statistical reckoning, the same writers and fans who revel in poetic description and conjure imagined worlds of play tend to be conversant with statistics and are aesthetically compelled by probability. Robert Coover's celebrated novel, *The Universal Baseball Association, Inc.*, published three years before the founding of the SABR and the dawn of sabermetrics, brought into public view baseball's twin obsessions with both literary imagination and strict bookkeeping. The novel's protagonist, J. Henry Waugh, is an accountant. He is also a literary creator who spins elaborate stories behind closed doors about fictional baseball players but constrains those stories with statistics and probability by methodically and scrupulously using dice to simulate athletic competition (Figure 12.1).

Baseball simulation is most familiar today in two nonliterary forms. On the one hand are video games that allow users to perform virtual versions of game actions—a genre of entertainment that is more popular for basketball, golf, and American football. Far more common in baseball is the kind of simulation known as fantasy sports, where fans play the part of executives and managers, rather than athletes, and compete based on the statistical performances of real players in real time. Modern fantasy baseball, which pioneered this mode of vicarious participation in spectator sports, began in the 1960s and spread in the 1980s with the emergence of rotisserie baseball (named for the French restaurant in New York where the original participants convened). In rotisserie, participants draft players in advance of a season and receive credit for their individual accomplishments.

As personal computers simplified scorekeeping and internet sites enabled competition among strangers, fantasy games became a multibillion-dollar business with tens of millions of participants worldwide across a range of spectator sports. Fantasy football (American) is especially popular, in part because a lighter schedule and specialization by position (a narrower range of players accrue statistics in each category) make participation less onerous, but fantasy baseball is also a major form of fan engagement.

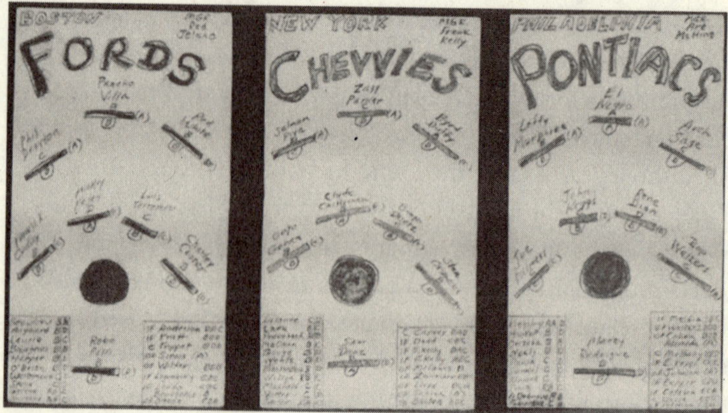

Figure 12.1 In 1935, the future Beat icon Jack Kerouac, then aged thirteen, created his own imaginary baseball league. Teams bore the names of automobile makes (the Philadelphia Pontiacs would face off against the Pittsburgh Plymouths) and fielded rosters of fictitious players, including a Cuban named El Negro (indicated here as the Pontiacs' centerfielder) who in 1935 would presumably have been barred from the white Major Leagues. Kerouac produced a deck of cards with which to simulate play, kept detailed statistical records, and even composed letters between owners discussing off-season trades. Kerouac continued to play the game until his death in 1969 but kept his league a private affair. *NYPL Berg Collection, Jack Kerouac Archive*

Although a significant portion of the business involves daily competitions for cash prizes (which are essentially the kind of traditional proposition bet that spectator sports have long attracted), fans who participate in longer-term fantasy leagues develop a rooting relationship to baseball that reshuffles traditional partisan loyalties while giving them a stake in many more games and many more events within the game. Whereas a Boston fan might once have cared only about games involving the Red Sox, perhaps tuning out if the team fell from contention, that same fan in a fantasy league now feels invested in players appearing in fifteen different games on a given night and in events as seemingly inconsequential as whether a particular relief pitcher enters the game in a position to get credit for what is somewhat arbitrarily defined as a *hold*.

Traditionalists may bemoan the distortions that this introduces to the fan experience, but in many respects fantasy baseball extends projects that have long been central to the sport: attending to long-term statistical trends, apportioning credit and blame to individual players in a team sport, and enlisting the spectator as an active, if vicarious, participant in someone else's athletic performance. All of these projects entail acts of radical imagination, one of several connotations of the term *fantasy*, which seems only appropriate. In that sense, fantasy baseball gratifies the longstanding literary impulse in baseball culture to imagine alternate universes.

At the same time, fantasy games highlight the dimension of baseball that is materialistic and commercial—not only because they are typically vehicles for wagering, but also because they turn fans into traders, reinforcing their identification with management and capital, rather than with heroic celebrity athletes. Here too, this does not mark a departure. Baseball as we know it is at core commercial entertainment, and projections of worker value have always been part of its discourse and spectacle.

None of this is unique to baseball because, in the end, baseball is not unique. Nor does it stand outside the dilemmas and conflicts that surround other entertainment forms or more obviously consequential pursuits. Instead, baseball has offered many people in various societies a complex and capacious space for thinking about such things as spectatorship, success, community, order, and contingency in the modern world. And to the extent that baseball matters, that would be the reason why.

Endnotes

Chapter 1

1. https://www.baseball-almanac.com/quotes/greg_maddux_quotes.shtml
2. Allen Guttman, *From Ritual to Record: The Nature of Modern Sports* (New York: Columbia University Press, 1978).
3. Jacques Barzun, *God's Country and Mine: A Declaration of Love Spiced with a Few Harsh Words* (Boston: Little, Brown, 1954), 159.
4. https://bleacherreport.com/articles/212819-when-baseballs-best-cultural-critic-turned-his-back-on-the-game
5. Quoted in Donald Hall, *Fathers Playing Catch with Sons: Essays on Sport (Mostly Baseball)* (Berkeley: University of California Press, 1985).

Chapter 2

1. Paul Goldberger, *Ballpark: Baseball in the American City* (New York: Knopf, 2019).

Chapter 3

1. Alexis de Tocqueville, *Democracy in America*, vol. 2, trans. Henry Reeve (New York: J. and H. G. Langley, 1840), 114–28.

Chapter 4

1. Ed Folsom, *Walt Whitman's Native Representations* (New York: Cambridge University Press, 1994), 47–48.
2. https://www.mlb.com/official-information
3. John Thorn, *Baseball in the Garden of Eden: The Secret History of the Early Game* (New York: Simon and Schuster, 2011), 71.
4. https://www.mlb.com/official-information

Chapter 5

1. Kenneth S. Greenberg, *Honor and Slavery: Lies, Duels, Noses, Masks, Dressing as a Woman, Gifts, Strangers, Humanitarianism, Death, Slave Rebellions, the Proslavery Argument, Baseball, Hunting, and Gambling in the Old South* (Princeton, NJ: Princeton University Press, 2020), 117–25.
2. Robert Whiting, *You Gotta Have Wa: When Two Cultures Collide on the Baseball Diamond* (New York: Knopf, 2009), 35.
3. Warren Goldstein, *Playing for Keeps: A History of Early Baseball* (Ithaca, NY: Cornell University Press, 1989), 44; Jules Tygiel, *Past Time: Baseball as History* (New York: Oxford University Press, 2000), 15–19.
4. Elliott J. Gorn, *The Manly Art: Bare-Knuckle Prizefighting in America* (Ithaca, NY: Cornell University Press 1986).
5. Tygiel, *Past Time*, 19.
6. Goldstein, *Playing for Keeps*, 38.
7. Jennifer Ring, *Stolen Bases: Why American Girls Don't Play Baseball* (Urbana: University of Illinois Press, 2009).

8. Albert G. Spalding, *America's National Game: Historic Facts Concerning the Beginning, Evolution, Development and Popularity of Base Ball, with Personal Reminiscences of Its Vicissitudes, Its Victories and Its Votaries* (New York: American Sports Publishing Co., 1911).
9. "Take Me Out to the Ballgame."
10. Stacey May Fowles, *Baseball Life Advice: Loving the Game That Saved Me* (Toronto: McClelland and Stewart, 2017); Payson quoted in Benjamin D. Lisle, *Modern Coliseum: Stadiums and American Culture* (Philadelphia: University of Pennsylvania Press, 2017), 108.
11. Ring, *Stolen Bases*.
12. Quoted in Erin C. Tarver, *The I in Team: The Secret History of the Early Game* (Chicago: University of Chicago Press, 2017), 171–72.

Chapter 6

1. John J. Harney, *Empires of Infields: Baseball in Taiwan and Cultural Identity, 1895–1968* (Lincoln: University of Nebraska Press, 2019), 22.

Chapter 7

1. Jules Tygiel, *Baseball's Great Experiment: Jackie Robinson and His Legacy* (New York: Oxford University Press, 1997), 13.
2. Harold Seymour, *Baseball: The People's Game* (New York: Oxford University Press, 1990), 549.
3. Tygiel, *Baseball's Great Experiment*, 15.
4. David Nasaw, *Going Out: The Rise and Fall of Public Amusements* (New York: Basic Books, 1993), 101.
5. Adrian Burgos Jr., *Playing America's Game: Baseball, Latinos, and the Color Line* (Berkeley: University of California Press, 2007), 36–46.
6. Michael Powell, "Curtis Granderson Is a Man on a Generous Mission," *New York Times*, November 28, 2016.
7. https://www.statista.com/statistics/1100127/interest-level-baseball-ethnicity

Chapter 8

1. Quoted in Roberto González Echevarria, *The Pride of Havana: A History of Cuban Baseball* (New York: Oxford University Press, 1999).

Chapter 9

1. Tygiel, *Past Time*, 65.
2. *The Sporting News*, April 27, 1922.
3. Roberto González Echevarria, *The Pride of Havana: A History of Cuban Baseball* (New York: Oxford University Press, 1999).
4. Tygiel, *Past Time*, 101; https://baseballhall.org/hall-of-famers/macphail-larry
5. From the podcast show "How to Do Everything," episode 93.
6. Carolyn L. Kane, *Electrographic Architecture: New York Color, Las Vegas Light, and America's White Imaginary* (Berkeley: University of California Press, 2023).

Chapter 10

1. John Fiske, "The Cultural Economy of Fandom," in Lisa A. Lewis (ed.), *The Adoring Audience: Fan Culture and Popular Media* (New York: Routledge, 1992), 41.

Chapter 11

1. Michael A. Fletcher, "Group Blocks Ty Cobb's Relative for Defending Negro Leagues Decision," ESPN, June 6, 2024, https://www.espn.com/mlb/story/_/id/40277219/cobb-gibson-negro-leagues-mlb
2. Tygiel, *Past Time*, 29.
3. Alan Schwarz, *The Numbers Game: Baseball's Lifelong Fascination with Statistics* (New York: St. Martin's Press, 2004), 167.
4. Michael Lewis, *Moneyball: The Art of Winning an Unfair Game* (New York: W. W. Norton, 2003).

Conclusion

1. Haruki Murakami, *Novelist as a Vocation* (New York: Knopf, 2022), 26–28.

Further Reading

Adair, Robert K. *The Physics of Baseball*, 3rd edition. New York: HarperCollins, 2015.

Angell, Roger. *The Summer Game*. Lincoln: University of Nebraska Press, 2004.

Baker, Kevin. *The New York Game: Baseball and the Rise of a New City*. New York: Knopf, 2024.

Barth, Gunther. *City People: The Rise of Modern City Culture in Nineteenth-Century America*. New York: Oxford University Press, 1982.

Barzun, Jacques. *God's Country and Mine: A Declaration of Love Spiced with a Few Harsh Words*. Boston: Little, Brown, 1954.

Block, David. *Baseball Before We Knew It: A Search for the Roots of the Game*. Lincoln: University of Nebraska Press, 2005.

Burgos, Adrian, Jr. *Playing America's Game: Baseball, Latinos, and the Color Line*. Berkeley: University of California Press, 2007.

Cavicchi, Daniel. "Fandom before 'Fan': Shaping the History of Enthusiastic Audiences." *Reception: Texts, Readers, Audiences, History* 6 (2014): 52–72.

Coover, Robert. *The Universal Baseball Association, Inc., J. Henry Waugh, Prop.* New York: Random House, 1968.

Fiske, John. "The Cultural Economy of Fandom." In Lisa A. Lewis (ed.), *The Adoring Audience: Fan Culture and Popular Media*. New York: Routledge, 1992.

Fletcher, Michael A. "Group Blocks Ty Cobb's Relative for Defending Negro Leagues Decision." ESPN, June 6, 2024.

Folsom, Ed. *Walt Whitman's Native Representations*. New York: Cambridge University Press, 1994.

Fowles, Stacey May. *Baseball Life Advice: Loving the Game That Saved Me*. Toronto: McClelland and Stewart, 2017.

Goldberger, Paul. *Ballpark: Baseball in the American City*. New York: Knopf, 2019.

Goldstein, Warren. *Playing for Keeps: A History of Early Baseball*. Ithaca, NY: Cornell University Press, 1989.

González Echevarria, Roberto. *The Pride of Havana: A History of Cuban Baseball*. New York: Oxford University Press, 1999.

Gorn, Elliott J. *The Manly Art: Bare-Knuckle Prizefighting in America*. Ithaca, NY: Cornell University Press, 1986.

Greenberg, Kenneth S. *Honor and Slavery: Lies, Duels, Noses, Masks, Dressing as a Woman, Gifts, Strangers, Humanitarianism, Death, Slave Rebellions, the Proslavery Argument, Baseball, Hunting, and Gambling in the Old South*. Princeton, NJ: Princeton University Press, 2020.

Guridy, Frank Andre. *The Stadium: An American History of Politics, Protest, and Play*. New York: Basic Books, 2024.

Guttman, Allen. *From Ritual to Record: The Nature of Modern Sports*. New York: Columbia University Press, 1978.

Hall, Donald. *Fathers Playing Catch with Sons: Essays on Sport (Mostly Baseball)*. Berkeley, CA: North Point Press, 1985.

Harney, John J. *Empire of Infields: Baseball in Taiwan and Cultural Identity, 1895–1968*. Lincoln: University of Nebraska Press, 2019.

Jacoby, Susan. *Why Baseball Matters*. New Haven, CT: Yale University Press, 2018.

Kane, Carolyn L. *Electrographic Architecture: New York Color, Las Vegas, Light, and America's White Imaginary*. Berkeley: University of California Press, 2023.

Kelly, William W. *The Sportsworld of the Hanshin Tigers: Professional Baseball in Modern Japan*. Berkeley: University of California Press, 2019.

Kingwell, Mark. *Fail Better: Why Baseball Matters*. Windsor, ON: Biblioasis, 2017.

Law, Keith. *Smart Baseball: The Story Behind the Old Stats That Are Ruining the Game, the New Ones That Are Running It, and the Right way to Think about Baseball*. New York: HarperCollins, 2017.

Lewis, Michael. *Moneyball: The Art of Winning an Unfair Game*. New York: W.W. Norton, 2003.

Lindbergh, Ben, and Sam Miller, *The Only Rule is it Has to Work: Our Wild Experiment Building a New Kind of Baseball Team*. New York: Henry Holt, 2016.

Lindbergh, Ben, and Travis Sawchik. *The MVP Machine: How Baseball's Nonconformists Are Using Data to Build Better Players*. New York: Basic Books, 2019.

Lisle, Benjamin D. *Modern Coliseum: Stadiums and American Culture*. Philadelphia: University of Pennsylvania Press, 2017.

Miller, Marvin. *A Whole Different Ballgame: The Inside Story of a Baseball Revolution*. New York: Ivan R. Dee, 2004.

Murakami, Haruki. *Novelist as a Vocation*. New York: Knopf, 2022.

Nasaw, David. *Going Out: The Rise and Fall of Public Amusements*. New York: Basic Books, 1993.

Noë, Alva. *Infinite Baseball: Notes from a Philosopher at the Ballpark*. New York: Oxford University Press, 2019.

Phillips, Christopher J. *Scouting and Scoring: How We Know What We Know about Baseball*. Princeton, NJ: Princeton University Press, 2019.

Prager, Joshua. *The Echoing Green: The Untold Story of Bobby Thomson, Ralph Branca and the Shot Heard Round the World*. New York: Pantheon, 2006.

Riess, Steven A. *City Games: The Evolution of American Urban Society and the Rise of Sports*. Urbana: University of Illinois Press, 1991.

Ring, Jennifer. *Stolen Bases: Why American Girls Don't Play Baseball*. Urbana: University of Illinois Press, 2009.

Roth, Philip. *The Great American Novel*. New York: Holt, Rinehart and Winston, 1973.

Ruck, Rob. *The Tropic of Baseball: Baseball in the Dominican Republic*. Lincoln: University of Nebraska Press, 1991.

Sahlins, Marshall, *Apologies to Thucydides: Understanding History as Culture and Vice-Versa*. Chicago: University of Chicago Press, 2004.

Schwarz, Alan. *The Numbers Game: Baseball's Lifelong Fascination with Statistics*. New York: St. Martin's Press, 2004.

Snyder, Brad. *A Well-Paid Slave: Curt Flood's Fight for Free Agency in Professional Sports*. New York: Viking, 2006.

Spalding, Albert G. *America's National Game: Historic Facts Concerning the Beginning, Evolution, Development and Popularity of Base Ball, with Personal Reminiscences of Its Vicissitudes, Its Victories and Its Votaries.* New York: American Sports Publishing Co., 1911.

Tarver, Erin C. *The I in Team: Sports Fandom and the Reproduction of Identity.* Chicago: University of Chicago Press, 2017.

Thorn, John. *Baseball in the Garden of Eden: The Secret History of the Early Game.* New York: Simon & Schuster, 2011.

Tygiel, Jules. *Baseball's Great Experiment: Jackie Robinson and His Legacy.* New York: Oxford University Press, 1997.

Tygiel, Jules. *Past Time: Baseball as History.* New York: Oxford University Press, 2000.

Voigt, David Quentin. *American Baseball: From the Gentleman's Sport to the Commissioner System.* University Park: Pennsylvania State University Press, 1983.

Walker, James R. *Crack of the Bat: A History of Baseball on the Radio.* Lincoln: University of Nebraska Press, 2015.

Whiting, Robert. *You Gotta Have Wa: When Two Cultures Collide on the Baseball Diamond.* New York: Knopf, 2009.

Williams, Blair. *Making Japan's National Game: A Cultural History of Baseball in Japan.* Durham, NC: Carolina Academic Press, 2021.

Yoder, April. *Pitching Democracy: Baseball and Politics in the Dominican Republic.* Austin: University of Texas Press, 2023.

Index